Clement and the Early Church of Rome

Clement and the Early Church of Rome

On the Dating of Clement's First Epistle to the Corinthians

~: **Reverend Thomas J. Herron** :~

Dissertatio ad Doctoratum
in Facultate Theologiae Biblicae
Pontificiae Universitatis Gregorianae

Rome 1988

~: **General Editor** :~
Scott Hahn

Emmaus Road Publishing
Steubenville, Ohio

Emmaus Road Publishing
1468 Parkview Circle
Steubenville, OH 43952

Printed in the United States of America
Second printing 2018

Library of Congress Control Number: 2008937980
ISBN: 9781931018470

Cover design by Julie Davis
Cover artwork: Twelfth Century Apsidal Mosaic of SS. Peter and Clement from the Church of St. Clement, Rome

Vidimus et approbamus ad normam Statutorum Universitatis
Romae, ex Pontificia Universitate Gregoriana
die 1 mensis iunii anni Domini 1987.

R.P. Prof. John Fuellenbach, S.V.D.
R.P. Prof. Ugo Vanni, S.J.

Imprimatur
John Cardinal Krol

Archbishop of Philadelphia
June 29, 1987

Clement and the Early Church of Rome:
On the Dating of Clement's First Epistle to the Corinthians

Appendix

Selected Bibliography

Foreword

It would be difficult to overestimate the historical value of Pope St. Clement's First *Epistle to the Corinthians*. It is one of the very few Christian documents that have survived from the generations immediately following the generation of the Apostles. The witness of those texts is rare and precious. They open a window on a world we wish to know, a world otherwise inaccessible. Tradition considers these witnesses collectively as the Apostolic Fathers, the first echo of the Apostles. For centuries, Christians took utmost care to preserve these writings, copying them out laboriously by hand and even risking their lives in order to hide them from persecutors. In the case of Clement's *Epistle to the Corinthians*, some local churches even preserved the book for veneration and proclamation, as part of the New Testament.

Since the early days of the Church, there has been an almost unanimous consensus about the authenticity and authority of the document. Still today, historians and theologians agree that it is a very early witness to the life of the Church. For reasons that Monsignor Thomas Herron makes clear, most scholars of the last century have placed the document at the end of the first century, around AD 96. But Msgr. Herron's meticulous research led him to conclude that the letter was composed much earlier, probably before AD 70. He was not the first scholar to argue for an earlier dating; John A.T. Robinson had done so, some decades before. But Msgr. Herron was the first scholar to undertake a thoroughgoing study of the matter.

His methods are rigorous. His writing is clear and unflinchingly honest. His tone is modest. Nevertheless, his conclusions are stunning. He argues very persuasively for the earlier dates; and then he proceeds to sketch out the significance of the early dating for history, theology, and apologetics.

Did he succeed? Well, his work has been cited as authoritative by scholars as illustrious as Cardinal Joseph Ratzinger. And His Holiness Pope Benedict XVI is certainly not alone.

One of the foremost experts on the Apostolic Fathers is Dr. Clayton Jefford of St. Meinrad School of Theology in Indiana. For more than a decade, his books have been the standard college and seminary textbooks on the Apostolic Fathers; and until recently he always favored a late date for Clement's *Epistle*. However, in his 2006 study, *The Apostolic Fathers and the New Testament*, he lays out all the possible dates and their respective arguments before he himself concludes: "I am ultimately content ... to place *1 Clement* in Rome, written by the hand of someone named

Clement (perhaps eventually to become Pope Clement) after the deaths of Paul and Peter (by tradition during the reign of Nero) but before the fall of the temple in the year 70." In a footnote, Dr. Jefford explains what caused his turnabout: "I am dependent here upon the brilliant analysis by Thomas J. Herron."

It is my pleasure and privilege to bring that "brilliant analysis" to a wider audience of scholars, as well as the growing number of lay readers who are interested in the Church Fathers.

My only regret is that I did not begin the process of publishing this book sooner. It was from the start a rare book, published in Rome in 1988 as the author's doctoral dissertation for the Pontifical Gregorian University. In the year after its publication, Father Herron presented his findings at the Oxford patristics conference, where it was received with excitement, and he published a summary in *Studia Patristica*. He planned to pursue the matter with further research, but God had other plans.

Msgr. Herron was summoned instead to serve as an official in the Vatican Congregation for the Doctrine of the Faith. For much of his time there, he was the English-language secretary to the prefect, Cardinal Ratzinger. Work at CDF is a more-than-fulltime job that leaves little leisure for historiography. But it was work that he loved. He later told his sister that the best part of the work was "working with Cardinal Ratzinger," who had become a "father figure" to the young Monsignor.

After serving his term, he returned to the Archdiocese of Philadelphia, where he served as a seminary professor, a newspaper columnist, and—his greatest delight—a pastor. He wrote weekly reflections on the lectionary readings that were soon picked up by a number of diocesan newspapers. He loved the families of St. Laurence Parish, and they loved him. And he continued his service to the Church as a theologian. Cardinal Ratzinger wrote him:

> "I am so grateful that in these years we have been able to stay in close contact, and I thank you from my heart for all the ways in which you have helped the Congregation since going back to America."

He continued to take correspondence and answer questions on his patristic research, but his priestly duties left him little time for research. He expressed the hope that he would return to Clement some day.

But it was not to be. In 2002 he was diagnosed with pancreatic cancer, from which he suffered mightily over the following months. His priest friends continued to go to him for confession. Bishops came to pay homage to a scholar and a friend. Archbishop Wilton Gregory wrote a moving account of their last meeting. He recalled that beside Msgr. Herron's bed was a letter from Cardinal Ratzinger, "one of the warmest, most comforting letters that I've ever read." It read, in part:

> "When I think of your time here in the Congregation it is your love for Christ's Church and your courage in the struggle to safeguard her saving truths that remain so vivid in memory.
>
> Your struggle now is of a different kind, but in some ways the same, since every action of a priest—if it is worthy of his priesthood—is a sharing in the sacrifice of Christ, that sacrifice which you have faithfully celebrated on the altar since the day of your ordination.
>
> The angels and saints are close to you in your illness, but know also that my thoughts and my prayers, especially at Holy Mass, accompany you."

Msgr. Herron died May 2, 2004, at age fifty-six.

He was eulogized on the editorial page of the *Wall Street Journal* by William McGurn, who was later the chief speechwriter for President George W. Bush. George Weigel credited Msgr. Herron with prophecy for predicting—in the face of universal skepticism—the elevation of his former boss to the papacy.

One of his last acts was to grant permission for us to reprint this valuable book. For that I am profoundly grateful. I wish also to express my gratitude to Msgr. Richard Malone, who helped us to work out the details.

I hope and pray that Msgr. Herron's book will now accomplish its mission, intended by the author and by God. May St. Clement intercede for us!

July 2008
The Year of St. Paul

Preface

The question arises naturally whether a specific study on the most probable date to be attributed to the first epistle of Clement to the Corinthians is warranted. Is it worth the trouble, from a theological point of view, to embark on an effort to examine all the relevant material which gives some indication of the mere date of a single Christian literary work which, while admittedly old, is not even considered to be part of the New Testament? The present thesis is, logically, an affirmative answer to the question and there are several reasons why. The first is that 1 Clement has emerged as a significant early Christian document in the contemporary theological discussion of Church order. First Clement is emphatically the first Christian author to be principally interested in the question of Church order and his lengthy treatment of the topic affords us a rare opportunity to understand at least some of the reasons why. But in the history of the systematic theological use of 1 Clement, it quickly becomes clear that it is not so much the text of 1 Clement that is decisive, but its date. That date, for 1 Clement, considered by Cullmann as "the document of ancient Christianity that can be dated with the greatest certainty,"[1] is almost universally accepted as being circa AD 95–96, and 1 Clement has thus become a landmark in the discussion of the early history of Church order because it is believed to give solid evidence concerning the state of church structure in the last decade of the first century. It is because its date has been considered such a key to the understanding of 1 Clement, and because that date is then used to bolster so much historico-theological argument, that this thesis will consider the matter in depth.

In Chapter One, the internal evidence for the date will be analyzed. In Chapter Two, an effort will be made to compare and contrast an early dating hypothesis with the external evidence available from the New Testament and from the early Patristic sources. In Chapter Three, a brief review of the possible consequences that an earlier 1 Clement would have for the interpretation of the letter itself will conclude with an effort to suggest some of the theological implications that an earlier date would have. In an Appendix, the external evidence for an "early" Clement will be considered.

It is hoped that this study will be of some help to those who wish to reflect on the contribution that 1 Clement makes to our knowledge of the early Church, to identify more clearly the precise tradition to which he

1 Oscar Cullmann, *Peter: Disciple, Apostle, Martyr* (New Haven: Meridian Books, 1958), 90.

is a witness. In the long term, perhaps such a study can also help assess more objectively the contemporary debate on the issue of ordained ministry in the Church as well since, above all, 1 Clement is preoccupied with the issue of presbyters in the Christian community at Corinth.

Reverend Thomas J. Herron
1987

Introduction
General Background of the Question

What is interesting about 1 Clement is that while it is a relatively rare example of first century Christian literature, its purpose and its ecclesiology are surprisingly clear. Since it explicitly says so, and there is no reason why the assertion should be doubted, 1 Clement was written in Rome and addressed to the Church in Corinth.[2] Similarly, we know that the letter was written because news reached Rome that certain presbyters had been removed from office in Corinth and the author insists that they be restored.[3] This somewhat obvious fact may help to see some other issues more clearly. It shows, for example, that there was already in Corinth a functioning presbyterate, and not a structureless, "charismatic" organization which some say was the more original style of Church life there. It will be a hotly contested point whether or not such an office can have existed at Corinth any earlier than the currently supposed date for 1 Clement, namely the middle nineties of the first century. Not specifically mentioned by Paul, presbyterate is sometimes viewed as a type of organizational model which some communities opted to introduce, and which later became universal in the Church, especially after hope in the early parousia began to fade. This late dating for any kind of structure in Christianity (sometimes generically called "Frühkatholizismus" or "Early Catholicism") has convinced many that 1 Clement, with all of its interest in presbyteral structure, cannot be any earlier than circa AD 95. In fact, some have preferred to date it well into the second century.[4]

Leaving aside for the moment *when* the epistle was written, since it explicitly calls for the *restoration* of a group of presbyters, one either has to conclude that the presbyterate had already existed in Corinth prior to the writing of the epistle, or that the epistle is a sheer fabrication, perhaps written by an author of the second century and fictitiously retrojected into the first century. This latter is the hypothesis of Eggenberger but has won very little scholarly support.[5]

On the supposition that 1 Clement is *not* fictional, though, one is struck by the fact that it so clearly portrays the presbyteral office as unacceptable to the Corinthian Church. In other words, 1 Clement is itself proof that there was in Corinth an ideological pluralism regarding Church office, its origin, and duration. It argues on behalf of a presbyterate principally because God has willed that the community of faith live in harmony and peace. It was for this reason

2 1 Clement, *Introduction*.

3 1 Clement 57:1–2.

4 Among these would be Barnikol, Delafosse, Eggenberger, Loisy, Merrill, Sturdy, and Turmel.

5 Cullmann, *Peter*, 90, no. 88: "This dating is connected with the much too one-sided perspective in which he (Eggenberger) regards the entire writing as an 'apology for the court'."

that the Apostles appointed presbyters and therefore the local Church is not now authorized to oust the presbyters and alter the apostolic order.

We may infer that the group pressing for the ouster succeeded, at least temporarily, and therefore must have had considerable sway in the community. It is impossible to say, however, how large the group was. First Clement seems to think they were small in number, one or two,[6] but 1 Clement's view may have been more rhetorical than real.[7] Perhaps he wanted to compliment the Corinthians with his judgment that surely those opposed to the presbyters were a distinct minority. It is possible that the group was more socially prominent than numerous. They may have been among those who lent their houses as places for community gatherings and exercised their influence that way.[8] Whatever the reason, this group succeeded in an ouster which probably had the support of many or most of the Corinthian Christians. All of this shows that 1 Clement's task is a grave and sensitive one, which will require consummate tact and clear and forceful argument if he is ever to have the presbyters reinstated.

Whatever one will eventually choose to say regarding the date, it should be recognized that we are faced here with an author of considerable theological acumen. His literary skills are evident, too, and the very size of the composition (65 chapters) is sufficient to show his ability to sustain a learned argument.

Regarding the ecclesiological viewpoint dominant in the letter, it has been widely shown that 1 Clement nowhere identifies himself as a single, "monarchical" bishop, nor does he call for monepiscopal government to be established or restored in Corinth, nor does he ask the Corinthian bishop's help in restoring order, something incomprehensible had there been a monepiscopate in place at Corinth at the time. The introduction of the letter which names its senders as "the Church of God which sojourns at Rome," the author's constant use of "we," his interchanging use of ἐπίσκοπος and πρεσβύτερος, and the fact that he never once appeals to the authority of his *office* as an argument in favor of accepting the ousted presbyters back, all of this points to the conclusion that we are dealing here with a piece of literature which antedates the emergence of a recognizable monepiscopacy.[9]

6 1 Clement 47:6.

7 Although this thesis is not itself indebted to what has been recently called "rhetorical criticism," here as at other points, the question of the rhetorical value of some of 1 Clement's assertions does deserve individual attention and study. Cf. George Kennedy, *New Testament Interpretation Through Rhetorical Criticism* (Chapel Hill: The University of North Carolina, 1984).

8 See Jerome Murphy-O'Connor, "St. Paul's Corinth: Texts and Archaeology," in *Good News Studies* 6 (Wilmington: M. Glazier, 1983), 158ff.

9 For a comprehensive view of the scholarly consensus, see John Fuellenbach, *Ecclesiastical Office and the Primacy of Rome: An Evaluation of Recent Theological Discussion of First Clement* (Washington, DC: Catholic University of America, 1980). He surveys the works of thirty-four scholars who commented on 1 Clement *ex professo*. Of these, *none* would hold for a date earlier than ca. AD 95–96, the vast majority agreeing with the ca. AD 96 fixing.

The question inevitably must be raised how it was that the author, if he was not a single bishop, nevertheless feels free to speak for the entire Roman church community. The simplest and, for the moment, most honest answer we have is that we do not know. We do not know because the epistle itself, expansive on many points as it is, does not explain the background of the decision to write to Corinth. It is not farfetched, however, to surmise that the author is himself one of the group of Roman presbyters. It may be that he had a reputation for literary composition and theological expertise, a reputation which the resultant 1 Clement would seem clearly to have justified, and that he was selected from the Roman presbyterate to author the letter for that reason. Still, the composition *could* have been a somewhat shared effort, with various individuals offering further points to be made, with the effect that the letter runs to its present length. The fact remains that the fourth century impression that the letter was the work of *a single bishop*, Clement, is not an interpretation demonstrably grounded in the text itself.

If this is so, if the author does not write as the single bishop of Rome, then the date of circa AD 95 is no longer tenable since that date rests on one simple piece of information, namely that Eusebius tells us that Clement of Rome was single bishop of Rome toward the end of the reign of the Emperor Domitian, whose death, we know, was in AD 96. Take away the belief that Clement wrote the letter known as 1 Clement *while he was bishop of Rome*, and the dating of circa AD 95 is seriously undermined. The issue is not whether Eusebius is correct about Clement's tenure as bishop, but whether that information has any possible relevance for the dating question. The irony is that although few today would admit that there is much evidence to support the idea that 1 Clement reflects monepiscopacy either at Rome or at Corinth, the majority of authors still seem content to allow the circa AD 95 date.

Even if the author of 1 Clement is not writing as *monepiskopos* of Rome, it is nonetheless clear that he expects what he says to be taken seriously. The demand that the ousted presbyters be reinstated is remarkable not simply because it is so blunt but also because it represents a hitherto unprecedented intervention of the Roman Church in the affairs of the Corinthian Church. Since 1 Clement does not reflect monepiscopacy at Rome, we are not probably dealing here with *papacy* properly so-called. This is because papacy implies monepiscopacy since the pope is the single bishop of Rome. Still, the intervention of 1 Clement is noteworthy, all the more so since, from all accounts, it was successful: the presbyteral structure was reinstated historically at Corinth, and remains there to this day.

The attribution of 1 Clement to Clement, sometimes called "Romanus," is universal, but exactly who this Clement was we have no idea.

The title, "The First Letter of Clement to the Corinthians," is used in every extant manuscript of the epistle.[10] It is clear, however, that the title does not origi-

10 A. Jaubert, *Clement de Rome: Epître aux Corinthiens*, 98, no. 1. For a full discussion of the

nate with its author but was attributed to the epistle in the subsequent manuscript tradition.

In fact, 1 Clement is technically anonymous since it identifies its senders only as "the Church of God which sojourns in Rome..."

Despite this, and although our knowledge of the historical Clement is quite limited, there seems to be little reason to doubt that Clement, whoever he was or whoever he later became, wrote the letter.[11]

The actual text, after being lost in the Middle Ages, was rediscovered with the Codex Alexandrinus, sent as a New Year's present by the Greek Patriarch of Constantinople, Cyril Lucar, to the English king, Charles I, in 1627. The Royal Librarian, Patrick Young, edited and published the two Clementine epistles contained in the codex, with modern chapter notation, in 1633.[12] It was this Young who surmised that 1 Clement was written in circa AD 95, a guess based on the above mentioned information from Eusebius, and confirmed by J.B. Lightfoot who published his influential '*Apostolic Fathers*,' which contains a massive commentary on 1 Clement, in 1879.[13]

In the Alexandrinus, 1 Clement was entitled KLEMENTOCE(PICT)OLH A'. It is followed by a Second Letter of Clement to the Corinthians, called "B." In the table of contents prefixed to the Alexandrinus by a scribe, it is listed under the heading, "HE KAINE DIATHEKE."

The Alexandrinus, however, lacks several folios and 1 Clement is missing about one tenth of its sixty-five chapters, a lacuna which extends from 57:6 to 64:1. It was not until 1875 that the remainder of the epistle was found and published. This was the accomplishment of Bryennios who found the Codex Constantinopolitanus in the library of the Patriarch of Jerusalem, at that time resident in Constantinople. The authenticity of this manuscript was in turn substantiated by the discovery of a Syriac version only a few months later in Paris in 1876. Finally, there exist two Coptic versions of the epistle, one from the fourth century the other from the eleventh or twelfth, as well as a Latin version, copied in the eleventh century from an original which could date from the second century, probably at Rome. The existence of these versions shows the wide importance attached to the epistle, and

manuscripts, see J. B. Lightfoot, *The Apostolic Fathers* vol. 1 (London: Macmillan & Co., 1898), 116–147.

11 Cf. Lightfoot, *The Apostolic Fathers*, vol. 1. Lightfoot's extensive analysis and effort to identify the historical Clement, pp. 14–103. For a very recent review of the question, cf. P. Lampe, *Die stadtrömischen Christen in den ersien beiden Jahrhunderten*, pp. 172–182. Lampe concludes, p. 182: "Alles in allem bleibt der individuelle Autor von 1 Clement trotz der Materialfiille merkwurdig im Dunkeln."

12 Trustees of the British Museum, *The Codex Sinaiticus and the Codex Alexandrinus*, ed. A. Jeffries Collins (London: The British Museum, 1951), 40.

13 Lightfoot, *Apostolic Fathers*, 1:34-6.

in the cases of the Alexandrinus and the later Coptic translation, that the epistle was even included in the New Testament.

As fortunate as their rediscovery was in the nineteenth century, the practical disappearance of manuscripts of 1 Clement from circulation after the eleventh century accounts for its lack of use among theologians in the Middle Ages and in the all-important Reformation period.[14] In turn, this may partially explain why Dr. Lightfoot's commentary, the first serious analysis made of 1 Clement after its complete rediscovery in 1875, has had such an enormous influence on subsequent scholarship. His work, and in particular his judgment that 1 Clement is to be dated to circa AD 95, has dominated the scholarly consensus since his time.

Nevertheless, the attribution of the work to Clement can and should be distinguished from the determination of its most probable date. In addition to the universal manuscript evidence, attribution to Clement can also be supported by other external indications.

The most important information about the identity of Clement comes to us from Eusebius Pamphilus of Caesarea in Palestine, who wrote his famous *History of the Church* sometime in the early fourth century. He states:

> After Titus had ruled for two years and as many months, his brother Domitian succeeded him. ... In the twelfth year of the same reign, Clement succeeded Anencletus.[15]

---

14 The Middle Ages were much more familiar with a collection of works now known as the Pseudo-Clementines. It is interesting to note that Saint Thomas Aquinas in the Prologue to his Commentary on the Epistle to the Hebrews, makes this amazing error: "*Unde dicebant ipsam esse vel Lucae Evangelistae, vel Barnabae, vel Clementis Papae; ipse enim scripsit Atheniensibus (!) quasi per omnia secundum stylum istum.*" A certain Angelus Pasqualis, bishop of Mottola, at the Council of Trent, in an undated relatio of February or March 1546, stated, "*Clemens in Epistola sua ad Corynthios (sic) meminit epistolae Pauli ad Hebraeos eiusque testimoniis utitur.*" (*Conc. Trid.*, vol. 9, p. 99. Cf. Eusebius, *HE* 3,38.) Likewise at Trent, at the general Congregation of November 7, 1562, Eustachius du Bellay, Archbishop of Paris, said, "*Quo vero ad questionem an episcopi lint de hire divino, Clemens ep.I dicit, episcopos esse Apostolorum successores a Christo institutos.*" It is not clear, however, that Eustachius had the actual text available: he is mistaken in applying what 1 Clement says about presbyters to the situation of bishops. Also, it is odd that such early testimony should not have had greater popularity among the Fathers at Trent (*Conc. Trid.*, vol. 9, p. 142).

15 Eusebius, *HE* 3,13,1–3,15,1: *dōdekatō de etei tēs autēs hēgemonias tēs Rōmaiōn ekklēsias Anenklēton etesin episkopeusanta dekaduo diadechetai Klēmēs.* Commenting on Eusebius, R. Grant in *Eusebius as Church Historian*, p. 5,7, has this to say: "In regard to the bishops of Rome, then, we conclude that Eusebius' dates are reliable only generally. That is to say that they fit in with what he knew and we know about the Church history of the 2nd and 3rd centuries. The names before Clement are open to question, as is the nature of the episcopate itself." Grant, p. 55, while identifying Irenaeus of Lyons as the source for Eusebius' Roman succession list, also notes that Irenaeus provided no *dates*. It was Eusebius' contribution, then, to align the particular bishops with the easily understood succession of Roman Emperors, the dates of whose accessions and deaths were certain since they were so much a part of the public record. The point of all of this is not to dispute Eusebius, but to receive the information he provides *on its own terms*: he identifies Clement as one who exercised the episcopate in the monepiscopal sense in which it was exercised

Because Eusebius specifically links the episcopacy of Clement with the reign of Domitian (AD 81–96), it is this text, more than any other single factor, which has resulted in the common assumption that 1 Clement is therefore to be dated in circa AD 95.

It should be mentioned, at least in passing, that this same Eusebius identifies Clement with the one mentioned in Paul's letter to the Philippians, 4:3.[16]

Eusebius also records that Dennis, bishop of Corinth around 170, wrote to the Romans and says that "ὑμῶν τὴν ἐπιστολήν" (apparently another letter from the Roman Church) is still being read at the celebration of the Lord's Day, and further notes that they likewise read the letter they had received "διὰ Κλή μεντος."[17]

Clement's association with this letter is also attested by Eusebius in a very curious passage quoted from Irenaeus of Lyons:

> It was in the time of this Clement that a serious revolt broke out among the brothers at Corinth. The Church at Rome sent a very important letter to the Corinthians to reconcile them in peace ...[18]

From this passage we can see the careful distinction made between the fact that the revolt took place "in the time" of Clement, but that it was "The Church at Rome" which sent the letter. This conforms exactly to what we know from the letter itself as was noted above. It reinforces, however, the tradition that Clement was the only individual associated with the letter.

In an anonymous work called the "Visions of the Shepherd," we have this additional account:

> Thou shalt therefore write two little books, and shalt send one to Clement and one to Grapte. For so shall Clement send to the foreign cities for this is his duty. (2.4.2 f.)

---

in Eusebius' own day. One can contest the historicity of this information if one likes, but the fact remains that even if Eusebius is correct, Clement would have to be a *monepiskopos* in ca. 96. If the Eusebian information itself is considered suspect, *a fortiori* there can be little justification in rejecting the historicity of the account while retaining the *Eusebian* connection drawn between Clement and Domitian.

16 Ibid., 3,15,1.

17 Ibid., 4,23,11. This external evidence is important to support the contention that the anonymous 1 Clement was in fact written by Clement. It is interesting to note that scholars, convinced of the Clementine authorship of 1 Clement, will not accept the Clementine authorship of 2 Clement, even though it, too, is anonymous, but uniformly attributed to Clement in the manuscripts which have survived. It should be recalled that, unlike 1 Clement, the author of 2 Clement speaks in the first person *singular*, and to that extent, sounds much more episcopal than the author of 1 Clement.

18 Ibid., 5,6,3.

Commenting on this passage, J.A.T. Robinson says:

> There is general agreement that unless this reference is a pseudonymous fiction (which there is no other reason to suppose) it must be to the Clement who was bishop of Rome in the last decade of the first century.[19]

While we can hardly be certain, the passage does seem to reflect a memory of Clement who wrote not as a bishop but because he was assigned to do so.

This "secretarial" role of Clement in writing the 1 Clement is a thesis proposed by J.B. Lightfoot as early as 1875. If accepted, it would allow us to see Clement as the author of the epistle, but at some point earlier than his putative episcopate at Rome in the mid-nineties. It is significant that Lightfoot, even though he maintained the 95 dating, still recognized that 1 Clement does not show any evidence of having been written by a *monepiskopos*.[20]

Therefore, it seems that there were ancient, independent sources which were unanimous in attributing this work to Clement. In fact, it is possible to say that the present *status quaestionis* regarding the authorship of the letter is likewise in favor of Clement. The question before us, however, is not *who* wrote 1 Clement, but *when* it was written.

Since modern scholarship is similarly agreed, with few exceptions, that 1 Clement was written in circa AD 95, it would be extremely repetitive here to review the many authors' arguments in favor of the common dating.[21] It may be charged, however, that while they may be in agreement about 1 Clement's date,

---

19 J. A. T. Robinson, *Redating the New Testament* (Westminster: John Knox, 1977), 320. Regarding the *Shepherd*, it has to be admitted that its author does indeed regard Clement as his contemporary. But since the *Shepherd*, too, is undated, it can hardly be used to claim that 1 Clement is of any particular period. Further study should be concentrated on this important aspect of the overall problem of the dating of paleochristian literature. Also, if the *Shepherd*'s "Clement" can presumably be identified with the Clement of 1 Clement, why could not one equally presume that he is the same as the Clement of Philippians 4:3? Robinson, pp. 319–322, shows well the complexities involved regarding the dating of the *Shepherd* and concludes in favor of a date within the first decade of Domitian's reign (81–91).

20 Lightfoot, *Apostolic Fathers*, 1:348.

21 Among the very few who do not agree with the prevailing consensus regarding 1 Clement's most probable date are the following. George Edmundson, in "The Church in Rome in the First Century," the Bampton Lecture, Oxford, 1913, gave a comprehensive argument for dating 1 Clement in ca. AD 70. A. E. Wilhem Hooijbergh in "A Different View of Clemens Romanus," in 1975, while not mentioning Edmundson's pioneering work, defended essentially the same position. John A. T. Robinson in *Redating the New Testament*, in 1976, sought to move all the New Testament, and with it 1 Clement, prior to AD 70. Robinson's effort has been met with considerable skepticism by contemporary scholars, among whom see Raymond E. Brown, in *The Churches The Apostles Left Behind*, p. 14, who dismisses Robinson's entire work as "maverick". Whether Robinson's arguments for dating the works of the New Testament are of equal merit with his observations on 1 Clement, is to be doubted. Still, each should be given the attention it individually deserves. To explain why Edmundson has not gained a wider following,

no commentator has as yet taken into account *all* the relevant textual evidence for establishing a date. Perhaps under the influence of the majority (practically unanimous since Lightfoot), perhaps because they wished to leave the scholarly consensus undisturbed for other reasons, modern authors have consistently referred to three or four passages in 1 Clement and have repetitively claimed to show that the circa AD 95 date is beyond doubt.

While it is true that *certainty* about the date of 1 Clement will always elude us, any hypothesis about its date can only be given the weight that the arguments advanced in its favor can sustain. The inherent contradiction in maintaining, on one hand, that 1 Clement shows no knowledge of monepiscopacy, and asserting, on the other, the relevance of Eusebius' dates for Clement's monepiscopacy at Rome for a probable dating of 1 Clement ought to be obvious. Either 1 Clement was written by a *monepiskopos* or it was not. Many of the same scholars who will conserve the circa AD 95 dating for 1 Clement are equally convinced that 1 Clement was not written by a *monepiskopos*. How can this contradiction be resolved?

This thesis will argue that there are 11 distinct instances, not of equal importance, wherein the text of 1 Clement itself will help to shed light on the dating question. They are listed here in the order of their appearance in the epistle together with a brief description of why each bears on the dating issue. All translations of 1 Clement, unless otherwise indicated, are by Kirsopp Lake, *Apostolic Fathers*, vol.1, Loeb edition.

1. 1 *Clement* 1:1

> "owing to sudden and repeated misfortunes and calamities which have befallen us ..."

This is usually taken to refer to the persecution of the Church thought to have been waged by Domitian, who reigned from AD 81-96.

2. 1 *Clement* 5:1

> "Let us come to those who contended in the days nearest to us: let us take the noblest examples of our own generation."

Here 1 Clement establishes some proximity between the deaths of the Apostles and his own day. The question is, how close a proximity?

3. 1 *Clement* 5:3*ff*.

> "Let us set before our eyes the good apostles: Peter ...Paul ..."

Robinson, *op. cit.*, p. 349, no. 4, suggests that the outbreak of World War I may have obscured his contribution and prevented its circulation in scholarly circles.

Related to the material in no. 2, here 1 Clement names Peter and Paul, whose deaths are fairly well dated to the pogrom at Rome under Nero in the years AD 64–67. This effectively establishes a *terminus a quo* for 1 Clement.

4. *1 Clement 7:1*

> "for we are in the same arena and the same struggle is before us."

This is often related to no. 1 as an indication that 1 Clement is alluding to the persecution of Domitian.

5. *1 Clement 40:1ff. and 1 Clement 41:2*

> "We ought to do in order all the things which the Master ordered us to do at appointed times. He commanded us to celebrate sacrifices and services, and that it should not be done thoughtlessly or disorderly, but at fixed times and hours. He has himself fixed by his supreme will the places and persons whom he desires for these celebrations in order that all things may be done piously according to his good pleasure ... for to the High Priest his proper ministrations are allotted, and to the priest, the proper place has been appointed, and on Levites their proper services have been imposed."

> "Not in every place, my brethren, are the daily sacrifices offered or the free will offerings, or the sin offerings and trespass offerings, but only in Jerusalem; and there also the offering is not made in every place but before the shrine, at the altar, and the offering is first inspected by the High Priest ..."

By far the lengthiest section of relevance to the dating question, and perhaps the most important, 1 Clement's reference to the Jerusalem Temple in the present tense is curious since Jerusalem with its Temple was destroyed under Vespasian, by his son Titus, in AD 70.

6. *1 Clement 44:3*

> "We consider therefore that it is not just to remove from their ministry those who were appointed by them (the Apostles) or later on by other eminent men."

First Clement apparently states that the Apostles themselves appointed some of the presbyters ousted by the Corinthians, but also that subsequent to the Apostolic appointment, there was an interim group appointed by others. It is argued that the circa AD 95 date would allow for this further development.

7. 1 Clement 47:3

"Even then you made yourselves partisans."

Alluding by name to Paul's First Letter to the Corinthians, 1 Clement charges his readers with continued partisanship. The question is whether, if 1 Clement were written in circa AD 95, he would have so directly accused that later generation of the shortcomings of their forebears.

8. 1 Clement 47:6

"the ancient Church of the Corinthians ..."

If 1 Clement were written prior to circa AD 95, would it have been appropriate to describe the Church of Corinth as "ancient"?

9. 1 Clement 63:3

"We have sent faithful and prudent men who have lived among us from youth to old age ..."

If 1 Clement were written prior to circa AD 95, would there have been sufficient time for these emissaries to have grown old "among us"?

10. 1 Clement 65:1

"Claudius Ephebus, Valerius Vito ..."

These two emissaries appear to have been the freed slaves of the household of the emperor Claudius, who died in AD 54, and his wife Valeria Messalina, who died in AD 48. If they were freed before the death of Claudius, and Roman law required that they be at least 30 years old to become citizens, would they not have been much too old in 95 to be sent as messengers to Corinth?

11. 1 Clement 65:1

"Fortunatus"

This third messenger is mentioned with no surname, suggesting, since the name itself was so common, that he was already known to the Corinthians. Could he be the same Fortunatus mentioned in Paul's 1 Corinthians 16:17? If so, would he not have been much too old in 95 to travel back and forth to Corinth on such a delicate mission?

No one of these issues is sufficient to date 1 Clement with certainty. Some of them may appear to the reader to be so minor as to be insignificant. The point, however, is that by taking them all into consideration, and realizing the weakness of the circa AD 95 date, a much earlier date becomes increasingly plausible.

Chapter One
The Internal Evidence

1.1 The Temple in Jerusalem (1 Clement 40:1–41:2)

It will be recalled that 1 Clement is an undated letter, that is, it nowhere makes reference to the name of the reigning Emperor or the consuls or the numbers of years since the foundation of the city of Rome. Any one of these references would have removed all doubt about the letter's actual date of composition. In a way, it is the absence of clear, datable references which has generated this entire discussion.

To say that 1 Clement did not avail himself of any of the conventional methods of Roman dating is not to imply in any way that this is unusual. It will be remembered, for example, that none of the several letters in the canon of the New Testament are explicitly dated. Although there may be majority opinions about the dates of given letters, the dating of those letters is also open to considerable debate, which in a way complicates our problem even further.

Nevertheless, when it is said that 1 Clement does not use dating references, this does not mean that there is no reference in the text to datable events. The single most important allusion is in 1 Clement 40, where Jewish sacrifices at the Jerusalem Temple are mentioned. No one disputes that Jerusalem and its Temple were destroyed in AD 70. If 1 Clement's date can be fixed in relation to the certain date of the fall of Jerusalem, there can be no surer or more reliable reference point.

The text of 1 Clement 40 is repeated here in its entirety:

> 1. Since then these things are manifest to us, and we have looked into the depths of divine knowledge, we ought to do in order all things which the Master commanded us to perform at appointed times. 2. He commanded us to celebrate sacrifices and services and that it should not be thoughtlessly or disorderly but at fixed times and hours. 3. He has himself fixed by his supreme will the places and persons he desires for these celebrations in order that all things may be done according to his good pleasure and be acceptable to his will. 4. So then those who offer their oblations at the appointed seasons are accepted and blessed, for they follow the laws and do no sin. 5. For to the High Priest his proper ministrations are allotted, and to the priests their proper place has been appointed and on Levites their proper services have been imposed. The layman is bound by the ordinances for the laity.

Chapter 41:

> 1. Let each one of us, brethren, be well pleasing to God in his own rank, and have a good conscience, not transgressing the appointed rules of his ministration, with all reverence. Not in every place, my brethren, are the daily sacrifices offered or the free-will offerings, or the sin-offerings and trespass-offerings, but only in Jerusalem; and there also the offering is not made in every place, but before the shrine, at the altar, and the offering is first inspected by the High Priest and the ministers already mentioned. 3. Those therefore who do anything contrary to that which is agreeable to his will suffer the penalty of death. 4. You see, brethren, that the more knowledge we have been entrusted with, the greater risk do we incur.

For a clearer and more complete analysis, the discussion of this passage is arranged in the following manner: first, the elements of the Greek text which merit particular attention and next, comments on the text which appear to support a revised dating hypothesis.

1.1.A *The Text*

40: 1. It is striking that the author blends a number of words which suggest order. "we ought to do *in order* all things" (*τάξει*); which the Master (*δεσπότης*) commanded (*ἐκέλευσεν*) us to perform at appointed (*τεταγμένους*) times."
2. "not disorderly (*ἀτάκτως*) but at fixed (*ὡρισμένοις*) times." Likewise, "he commanded (*ἐκέλευσεν*)."
3. The sense of order or command continues in the verb *θέλει*, here however in the *present* tense. The verb "he fixed (*ὥρισεν*)" reverts to the aorist tense. God's will is supreme (*ὑπερτάτῃ*).
4. The main verb, "they sin (*διαμαρτάνουσιν*)" is in the present. The seasons are described as "appointed (*προστεταγμένοις*)," a perfect participle.
5. The verbs change to the perfect tense: *δεδομέναι εἰσί*, *προστέτακται*, *δέδεται*, side by side with a present, *ἐπίκεινται*.

41: 1. The order motif is continued: "... in his own rank (*τάγματι*) ..."; "the appointed rule (*τὸν ὡρισμένον κανόνα*)."
2. The present tenses here are more noteworthy: the sacrifices "are offered (*προσφέρονται*)"; the offering "is made (᾿)."

The various types of Jewish sacrifice are distinguished: daily sacrifices, free-will offerings, sin-offerings and trespass-offerings.

The Temple area is not described vaguely or generically, but precisely: "before the shrine (ἔμπροσθεν τοῦ ναοῦ), at the altar (πρὸς τὸ θυσιαστήριον)."

Likewise, the specific responsibility of examining the sacrificial offering by the High Priest (ἀρχιερέως) is recognized.

1.1.B *Commentary*

Since the date of the destruction of the Jerusalem Temple is for all practical purposes certain, establishing a link between the text of 1 Clement and that destruction is essential. It is not going too far to say that the position one takes regarding this passage in 1 Clement will largely determine one's overall view about the date. It's important for this study, then, cannot be overemphasized.

Attention has been drawn above to the fact that, throughout this section, repeated reference is made to *divinely willed order*. This emphasis is a *leit-motif* for the entire epistle since 1 Clement's whole point is that the *dis*order currently rampant in the Corinthian Church is repugnant to God's will. To sustain this point 1 Clement continually draws attention to other forms of divinely willed order (as in chapter 20, where he speaks of the heavens, the sea, the seasons, and the animal kingdom, and concludes (20:11), "All these things did the great Creator and Master of the Universe ordain to be in peace and concord ..." In chapter 33, he practically repeats the same material. In chapter 37, leaving divinely willed order, he makes a more commonsense appeal to consider the order necessary for the army to exist and to function properly (37:3,4): "Not all are prefects, nor tribunes, nor centurions, nor in charge of fifty men or the like, but each carries out in his own rank the commands of the Emperor and of the generals. The great cannot exist without the small, nor the small without the great; there is a certain mixture among all, and herein lies the advantage." There follows an extended simile based on the human body, clearly, if not surprisingly, echoing the thought of Saint Paul in 1 Corinthians 12:12ff.[22]

There can be no question, then, that 1 Clement makes use of the reference to the Jerusalem Temple for a definite purpose: to argue to the need for similar order in the Church of God at Corinth.

That said, three major issues emerge in the analysis of this material which shall have to be confronted. One is the use of the present tenses throughout the section. Another is whether there is any contradiction in maintaining that

22 There is an intriguing possibility that 1 Clement's reference was, at least in part, inspired by Paul's reference to the Temple in 1 Corinthians 9:13–14: "Do you not know that those who are employed in the Temple service get their food from the Temple, and those who serve at the altar share in the sacrificial offerings? In the same way, the Lord commanded that those who proclaim the gospel should get their living by the gospel." We are certain from 1 Clement 47 that he knew the canonical 1 Corinthians. Although their arguments are quite different, the similar manner of argumentation by reference to Temple practice seems clear. But, of course, the Temple was standing when Paul wrote 1 Corinthians! See Donald A. Hagner, *The Use of the Old and New Testaments in Clement of Rome* (Boston: Brill Academic, 1997), 197ff.

Jerusalem is the only place to offer sacrifices, while at the same time considering in 44:4 that the Christian presbyters had "blamelessly and holily offered its (of the episcopate) sacrifices." A third is whether or not sacrifices might still have been being offered in Jerusalem in the middle 90's.

Naturally, when the verb is in the present tense, the normal meaning is that the action described by the verb is contemporaneous with the time of the composition. An exception is the historical present whereby a present tense can be used to describe an action already passed at the time of the composition.

Obviously, if 1 Clement used present tenses to describe the action of the offering of sacrifices in the Jerusalem Temple, which everyone acknowledges to be lying in ruins in the 90's, either those tenses are normal or historical. If they are normal, they would imply that Temple sacrifice was continuing, and known to be continuing, at the time of the composition. If historical, then 1 Clement would simply mean that once upon a time such sacrifices were offered, but not necessarily any longer.

Lightfoot, as we have seen, was persuaded that 1 Clement was written in the 90's and therefore chose to read these present tenses as historical. He cited a passage in Flavius Josephus (*Contra Apionem* 2,77) in which that author, long after the Temple lay ruined, used present tenses to describe the Jewish sacrifices.[23]

Now, there can be no doubt that such a thing as an atemporal or historical present exists, and in fact was quite common in Hebrew, Aramaic, Greek, and Latin. It exists in English. The question is how to decide whether these present tenses are normal or not.

The first indication that a present tense refers to a particular time is the context within which it is used. When it is clear that the past is meant, then the historical use of the present tense presents no particular difficulty. Still, it must be admitted that the text itself should give the reader some kind of clear indication that the author does not intend to use the present tense in the normal way.

The principal reason for using the historical present is to render a passage more vivid, especially in a narrative where the author imagines himself present.[24]

In post-classical Greek there was an increasing tendency to use the historical present for discourses with verbs of speaking, e.g., λέγειν, with verbs of seeing and with verbs of motion, especially coming and going.[25]

---

23 Lightfoot, *Apostolic Fathers*, 1:353. Cf. Raymond E. Brown and John P. Meier, *Antioch and Rome: New Testament Cradles of Catholic Christianity* (Mahwah: Paulist, 1983), 169, no. 360. It will be noticed that Brown is so convinced that 1 Clement uses the historical present, p. 150, that he cites 1 Clement to show that the present tenses in Hebrews 8, 9, and 10 are also historical.

24 James Hope Moulton, *A Grammar of New Testament Greek* (Edinburgh: T. & T. Clark, 1963), 60.

25 Ibid., 61; see also F. Blass and A. Debrunner, *A Greek Grammar of the New Testament* (Grand Rapids: Zondervan, 1976). The question of the historical present is certainly complex. I would personally prefer to speak, not of the normal or the historical present, but of the temporal or atemporal use of the present tense. Strictly speaking, what has been called the *historical*

As we view the instances of these present tenses in this section of 1 Clement, it does not appear that the argument for their being historical presents is very strong.

If anything, the entire context of the lengthy argument of 1 Clement for order would suggest that he is again appealing to what he can show to be an actual example of such order, as he had when he referred to the body, the army, the seasons, and nature in general. The entire thrust of his argument is "just as ... so too ..." He uses past examples of human behavior (with past tenses!) when he cites the Old Testament to show that similar virtuous behavior is expected of contemporary believers as it has always been expected in the past. But he admits this when he says, 5:1: "But, to cease from the examples of old time ..." The principal point here, however, is that 1 Clement's examples from the Old Testament are *people*, who must necessarily some day die. The fact that they died, i.e., are not liv-

---

present is a usage which has nothing to do with time: it is used for some other motive, perhaps for vividness, perhaps for mere variety, e.g. 1 Clement 17:4: "But Job accuses (κατηγορεῖ) himself, saying ...", where it is used to introduce a Scriptural text even though it is obvious that the text is ancient and Job is long since deceased. Nevertheless the terminology "historical present" is by now conventional.

In his famous *Griechische Grammatik*, pp. 271ff., E. Schwyzer distinguishes the *historical* present from the *dramatic* present, used for example in Aeschylus's play, *The Persians*, 299–515. As already noted, an author who is using the present tense *not* to signify contemporaneous action but as a *praesens pro praeterito* must give his readers some indication that this is the case. Sometimes the clue is logical, as when the switch to the present tense occurs in a narrative using past tenses, or the clue may be contextual, as for example in a play. When the action is happening on a stage for all to see, if an actor uses a present tense to describe something that is *not* occurring at that moment, it may safely be deduced he is using what Schwyzer called the dramatic present. When, in *The Persians*, a messenger enters to describe the horrors of a previous defeat of the Persian fleet and uses present tenses to do so, the audience is conscious of the fact, and the dramatic use of the *praesens pro praeterito* creates the desired effect of increased vividness in the narrative.

C. Osborn in "The Historical Present in Mark as a Text Critical Criterion," distinguishes three uses: p. 496: a "cataphoric" use of isolated historical presents within units dominated by past tense verbs to denote a semantic shift within the account to material of a somewhat different nature, e.g., Mark 1:29–34; p. 498, the use of the historical present to set the stage for an event, with the account given in past tense verbs, e.g., Mark 1:21; and p. 498, the use of the historical present to mark the main features of a discourse, culminating in each instance in past tense verbs. Osborn clearly makes the point that, in a quasi "historical" or at least narrative format, which the gospels are by definition, several uses of the present tense can be distinguished. Our problem in 1 Clement is that it is not, in general, a narrative but an exhortation. His references to the Temple are not narrative descriptions, but have a clear exemplary and hortatory purpose.

H. St. John Thackeray, in *The Septuagint and Jewish Worship: A Study in Origins* (Germantown, NY: Periodicals Service Company, 1923) p. 21, posits that the historical present can function "to introduce a date, a new scene, a new character, occasionally a new speaker, in other words, a fresh paragraph in the narrative." The common element in all of these analyses of the use of the historical present *is* that it be used in some kind of *narrative, that* it be, in other words, historical. This is simply not the case in 1 Clement's description of the Temple.

ing examples of virtue, does not alter his argument that just as they were, so should the Corinthians be. When he speaks of order, though, he is appealing to enduring and perennially valid examples of order, e.g., nature or the army. Applying this to his reference to the Temple, one would have to admit that if the Temple, once quite an ordered affair, now lay in ruins, 1 Clement would have been better advised not even to mention the Temple in the first place.

Further, Lightfoot, when he appeals to Josephus' usage to show that 1 Clement may be using the historical present as well, ignores two important points. One, Josephus is recognized to be the ancient author who used the historical present the most.[26] Second, in reading Josephus, especially regarding the destruction of the Temple, we take into account the fact that it was none other than Josephus who tells us of the sack of the Temple and that, therefore, it is certainly an historical present. In other words, what we already know of Josephus and the dates of his works forms a kind of context in which we easily see that his present tenses are not normal, but historical. Much the same may be said of the Jewish compilers of the *Mishnah*: while it is true that, long after its destruction, the Temple is still spoken of in the present tense (e.g., Berakoth 1.1), we know *that the compilers knew* that the Temple was no more (e.g. Tannaith 4.6). One may speculate on the reasons why the compilers used the historical present: perhaps it was a pious manner in which the Temple's actual destruction, such a painful fact to the Jewish faithful, need not be directly admitted. We shall never know. Suffice it to say, however, that there is no possible question that the *Mishnah* itself was formed after the Temple's destruction, but its present tense description of the already ruined Temple remains coherent. One simply cannot say that of 1 Clement: we do *not* know that 1 Clement knows the Temple is in ruins! One may conclude therefore that on the basis of context, one not only cannot prove that 1 Clement's presents are atemporal, in fact the context of his argument for order makes it probable that he is referring to examples of order contemporary to him as he wrote, and therefore normal present tenses. His careful specification, in 41:2, of four different types of Jewish sacrifices being offered in the Jerusalem Temple only enhances the impression that he is referring to actual contemporary practice.

But the argument against the historical present is even stronger. As already noted, it is often found in passages where the narration is deliberately put in the present tense for vividness. First Clement is not involved here in a narrative. If he describes the action, his description is not for description's sake, but to illustrate the order of the ensemble, location, action and persons combined. Moreover, he does not introduce the passage as part of a discourse or in which he imagines himself to be present.

26 Moulton, *Grammar of New Testament Greek*, 61.

The argument of Lightfoot et al. that this passage is irrelevant to a determination of the date of 1 Clement since its present tenses are historical is thus weak indeed.

A second problem which could appear to present difficulties to the thesis that 1 Clement is referring to sacrifices still being offered in the Jerusalem Temple as he wrote is the fact that in 44:4 he does acknowledge that the Christian elders who had been ejected from Corinth were seen to be offering the "sacrifices" of the episcopate. Since in 41:2, he had said that God had required the sacrifices to be offered "in Jerusalem alone (μόνη)," how can 1 Clement then speak of other Christian "sacrifices"?

To resolve this apparent contradiction, several things must be kept in mind. The first is that, within the context of the Old Testament itself, even where the ritual offering of sacrifices is exclusively reserved to the Temple, the Psalmist could still speak of two different "sacrifices":

> Thou hast no delight in sacrifice;
> if I brought thee an offering, thou wouldst not accept it.
> My sacrifice, O God, is a broken spirit;
> a wounded heart, O God, thou wilt not despise. (Psalm 51: 16–17)

As we have seen, 1 Clement 41:2 specifies four different kinds of sacrifices that are to be offered in the Temple: the daily sacrifices, the free-will offerings, the sacrifices for sins and for trespasses. He states that these are to be offered in Jerusalem "alone," but it does not follow that the sacrifices of the episcopate, whatever is meant by the term, would be included in those sacrifices which had to be offered in the Temple, but, like the Psalmist's sacrifice, could easily be offered elsewhere, without prejudice to the official cult.

Finally, we have reliable indications that the early Christians continued to frequent the Temple. We do not know with certainty that they continued to offer sacrifices there, although there is no *a priori* reason why they should not have, so long as the Temple stood. While the sacrificial nature of the Eucharist and the fact that it replaces the Temple cult would not have been understood by all from the beginning, we will see below that Hebrews, prior to the Temple's destruction, could already begin to conceive of Jesus as the high priest. Thus, the events of AD 70 were not necessary for Christians to begin to examine the sacrificial aspects of their own cult. At the same time, Christian converts from Judaism were free to practice all the aspects of the Temple worship, including sacrifice, while the structure for the cult was still intact.

All of this is to argue that reference in 1 Clement 44:4 to the sacrifices of the episcopate does not contradict the author's insistence that certain sacrifices were still to be offered in Jerusalem, and there alone.

To these considerations must be added the historical question: granting *arguendo* that these present tenses are not clearly historical, could it be that 1 Clement, writing in the 90's, is in fact alluding to the Jewish cult which had been continued, in accordance with the divine will, even after the destruction of Jerusalem in AD 70? The question is admittedly intriguing.

K.W. Clark, writing in 1960, raises this precise issue.[27] He argues that after previous destructions of the Temple, pious Jews maintained the Temple cult despite the crumbled state of the buildings. The very fanaticism which had led to the Jewish revolt in 66 and resulted in the destruction of the Temple, would have continued to fuel the piety of the survivors. So much so that "only one factor could bring the Jews to cease such worship and that would have been the physical prevention imposed upon them."[28] No one can prove that the Romans were successful at physically preventing the surviving Jews from practicing their ancient cult, so, Clark concludes, it must be held probable that in some way they did so.

Clark's thesis has significant implications for our study and so a somewhat detailed analysis of his position is called for.

Several background historical factors should be kept in mind. One is that the destruction of the city and the Temple area was quite thorough. We know this from Flavius Josephus, a Jewish priest refugee from the destruction, who becomes a Roman historian and finds a literary patron in Titus, the victorious conqueror of Jerusalem, son of the reigning Emperor Vespasian, and himself Vespasian's successor.[29]

While it is true that Josephus' account of the Jewish War is not entirely without shortcomings and personal interest (what author's isn't?), it is also true that he has documented the precise period of the destruction of Jerusalem in an extraordinary way. His account of the wholesale carnage which ensued upon Titus' taking of Jerusalem in 70 is supported in recent archeological study, not available to Clark when he wrote. Kathleen Kenyon conducted extensive archeological digs in the present Old City of Jerusalem and in the area immediately adjacent to the Temple and published her findings in 1974. She writes:

> The ensuing slaughter and destruction were terrible. There is ample archeological evidence of the destruction. The most dramatic was in Site N. ... In the ruins, churned up by winter torrents, were human bones, including three skulls, a reminder of the slaughter described by Josephus, which filled the streets with blood. In Site K, on the terrace above, human bones were also found in the drain that ran beneath the first century house.

27 Kenneth W. Clark, "Worship in the Jerusalem Temple After A.D. 70," *New Testament Studies* 6 (1959–60): 269–80.

28 Ibid., 271.

29 Tessa Rajak, *Josephus* (London: Gerald Duckworth, 1983), 4, *et passim.*

> The most striking evidence here, however, is that with the destruction of this house, occupation in this part of Jerusalem comes to an abrupt end.[30]

What Miss Kenyon's findings seem to indicate is that the entire section of Jerusalem around the Temple mount was completely abandoned.

After the destruction of AD 70, she asserts, no further signs of human inhabitation were found, something unlikely if, as Clark would hold, the Temple mount was the site of continued Jewish cultic practices until its definitive destruction in 131 under Hadrian. But Miss Kenyon's find is actually more significant: since she found human bones scattered throughout the level which she identified as that of the AD 70 destruction, it means that those bones were left to lay in their disheveled state in the environs of the Temple. Clark's hypothesis of Jews returning after AD 70 to continue the Temple cult would thus have to allow for the fact that none of these same Jews bothered to remove these remains for proper burial, and that their continued presence in the environs of the Temple mount did not render the Temple area itself ritually unclean and hence unusable. But his entire point is that the Jews who survived were so pious that they would surely have continued the cultus unless actively impeded. It seems equally probable that their very piety would have compelled them to bury the dead. The fact that they manifestly did not do so, or perhaps were prevented from doing so, undermines Clark's entire view. Further we know from archeological sources that the Tenth Roman Legion "Fretensis" was stationed alongside the Temple area.[31]

Again, to quote Miss Kenyon:

> When the sack of Jerusalem was completed, Titus left the Xth Legio Fretensis to watch over the ruins. Some Jews continued to live in Jerusalem, but the tragic difference was that there was no longer a Temple in which the full ceremonial of the worship of Yahweh could be carried out. Religious ceremonies continued, but in synagogues, with the forms of service suitable for those who had no access to the Temple. A new form of Judaism grew up, under the guidance of the priestly Sanhedrin, now established at Jamnia in the coastal plain, concerned with the interpretation of the Scriptures.[32]

Kenyon is referring to the more reliable findings that while there is some indication of inhabitation of Jerusalem elsewhere than in the Temple area (the

30 Kathleen Mary Kenyon, *Digging up Jerusalem* (New York: Doubleday Benn, 1974), 254.

31 Stevenson and Momigliano, *Cambridge Ancient History* vol. 10 (Cambridge: Cambridge University), 863.

32 Kenyon, *Digging up Jerusalem*, 256.

very presence of the Roman Legion being one example), the more pious Jews, the ones Clark would have continuing the cultus, in fact had migrated under the leadership of one Johanan ben Zakkai to Jamnia or Jebneh where Vespasian had allowed him and the more moderate Jews to establish a rabbinic school.[33] These were pious Jews but they abandoned Jerusalem and its Temple. Perhaps a reason for this abandonment, beside the fact that the Romans were obviously interested in preventing any recurrence of the Jewish rebellion just ended, and so treated the politically moderate Jews with some deference, is the steady erosion of respect for the High Priesthood and the Temple cultus itself in the period just prior to the rebellion itself.[34] Clark thinks that the Jews would at all costs have continued the Temple services but ignores the fact that for years, especially among the more pious, those Temple services came under continual criticism.[35] The Essene community is an example of how pious Jewry could reject the Jerusalem Temple. The fact that ben Zakkai moved to Jamnia, and a whole group of his followers with him, is likewise evidence that the geography of Jerusalem and its Temple were of less and less consequence to the religiously inclined survivors of the disaster of AD 70.

But to return to 1 Clement: the question has been raised whether 1 Clement might in fact be referring to a religious practice which had endured into the 90's.

First of all, those that accept this solution must logically admit that the verbs used are not historical presents.

Secondly, there is serious reason to doubt the likelihood of Clark's hypothesis.

Thirdly, and perhaps most importantly, 1 Clement describes a scene of ritual order which he makes part of his argument for order in the Corinthian Church. Clark's hypothesis, even if possible, instead conjures up a vision of a pathetic and furtive re-enactment of Israel's ancient rites among the fallen walls and broken columns of a once proud and awesome Temple. This is hardly 1 Clement's reference. He specifies four different types of sacrifices offered in the Temple. He refers explicitly to the ναός and the θυσιαστήριον.[m] The golden table of Showbreads from the Temple had long since been carried away as part of Titus' spoils. The

33 Rijak, *Josephus*, 188–189; see also, A. J. Saldarini, "Johanan ben Zakkai's Escape from Jerusalem," *Journal for the Study of Judaism in the Persian, Hellenistic, and Roman Period*, 6 (1975): 189–204.

34 Even the schismatic Temple at Leontopolis in Egypt was closed in AD 73 , although already in decay, in order to prevent its becoming a center of attraction after the closing of the Jerusalem Temple. Cf. Stevenson and Momigliano, *Cambridge Ancient History*, vol. 10, p. 864. See also, *Cambridge Ancient History*, vol. 8, p. 517.

35 J. Alberto Soggin, *A History of Israel* (London: SCM, 1984), 322: "Because in the past the Temple had too often been the center of intrigue and collaboration with the occupying forces, it had lost much of its prestige even before the catastrophe; that explains why there was virtually no thought of rebuilding it, though that had been a priority for those returning from exile in the second half of the sixth century B.C."

sacking itself is shown in the bas-relief of the Arch of Titus, erected in the Roman Forum shortly after Titus' death in AD 81, and still on view today.[36]

Therefore, the argument that 1 Clement is using historical present tenses to describe the no longer extant Temple cult is very weak. Weak too, is the counter thesis that somehow the cultus was continued in 1 Clement's own day. It will be shown later that this very positive reference to the Temple cult is innocent of the anti-Temple polemics which characterize much of the New Testament. For the present, though, it is sufficient to observe that, objectively, the Temple references in 1 Clement are worthy of more serious consideration than they have been given in determining the most probable date of its composition.

To repeat: no one issue is of itself going to be determinative, but it must be admitted that the very datable destruction of Jerusalem shall have to figure significantly in any plausible dating hypothesis.

1.2 The Alleged Persecution Under Domitian (1 Clement 1:1)

The second most important text of 1 Clement to consider which bears directly on the dating of the letter is 1 Clement 1:1:

> *Διὰ τὰς αἰΦνιδίους καὶ ἐπαλλήλους γενομένας ἡμῖν συμφορὰς καὶ περιπτώσεις*

> K. Lake translates this as:

> "Owing to the sudden and repeated misfortunes and calamities which have befallen us."

> Regarding the persecution of Domitian, Lake has this to say:

> If it be assumed that chapter 1, which speaks of trouble and perhaps of persecution, refers to the time of Domitian, it can probably be dated as circa AD 96; but we know very little about the alleged persecution in the time of Domitian and it would not be prudent to decide that the epistle cannot be written ten or fifteen years later.[37]

> A. Jaubert translates 1:1 as:

---

36 Josephus in BJ VII, V, 122–156, describes the triumph of Titus after his return from Jerusalem: "The spoils were borne in promiscuous heaps; but conspicuous above all stood out those captured in the Temple at Jerusalem. These consisted of a golden table, many talents in weight, and a candelabrum, likewise made of gold."

37 K. Lake, *The Apostolic Fathers* vol. 1 (London: Macmillan & Co., 1898), 5.

> A cause des malheurs et des calamités qui nous sont survenus subitement coup sur coup.[38]

Though she cites the tradition according to which such a description might fit the supposed persecution of Domitian, she prefers to base her calculations of the date on other texts. In fact, she admits,

> Mais it ne semble pas qu'il y ait eu de persécution directe contre les chrétiens.[39]

In a recent article (1984), L.L. Welborn provides the most extensive and detailed analysis yet done of the question of whether 1 Clement 1:1 should be taken as a reference to a persecution of the Christian community in Rome by the Emperor Domitian.[40] Needless to say, if such a link to Domitian *were* to be established securely, a *terminus a quo* of at least AD 81, the year of his accession, would be proven for the composition of 1 Clement.

While indebted to Welborn, and dependent on his work on 1:1, the present study is in serious disagreement with some of his observations. Various points of disagreement will be pointed out as they arise, but specifically here, he claims that "confidence in the received date of AD 95–96 is based on a single verse," i.e. 1:1.[41] This is not the case. There is general agreement, despite the fact of the technical anonymity of the epistle, that 1 Clement was written by Clemens Romanus and that this Clemens is the same individual Eusebius described as becoming bishop of Rome "in the twelfth year ... of the reign" of Domitian.[42] One need not quarrel with this identification of Clemens but it should be seen that the dating comes, not from interpreting 1:1 as persecution, but from connecting such persecution with *Domitian*, information which essentially derives from the reference of Eusebius and not from the text of 1 Clement itself. More important for the AD 95–96 date is Eusebius' report that Clement was bishop of Rome toward the end of Domitian's reign. This information is then projected onto the text of 1 Clement, v. 1:1 is interpreted as persecution, and therefore it must be *Domitian's* persecution, etc.

38 Jaubert, *Epître aux Corinthiens*, 99.

39 Ibid., 19, no. l.

40 L. L. Welborn, *On the Date of First Clement*, 35–54. See also, R. L. P. Milburn, "The Persecution of Domitian," *Church Quarterly Review* 139 (1945): 154–164; G. Brunner, *Die theologische Mitte des ersten Klemensbriefes*, 101, 142–143. But contra, L. W. Barnard, "St. Clement of Rome and the Persecution of Domitian," in *Studies in the Apostolic Fathers and Their Background*, 15: "Domitian was not a wholesale 'persecutor' of the Church as Nero was. ... However, Domitian's persecution was a succession of short, sharp, assaults. ..."

41 Ibid., 38.

42 Eusebius, *HE* 3,15. See above, no. 15.

Welborn's reluctance even to admit that the verse refers to persecution at all is nevertheless quite to the point. He shows that E.T. Merrill in 1920 already questioned the reference to persecution in 1:1:

> The language does not suggest to an unprejudiced eye that anything very terrible has shaken the Roman Church. It sounds curiously like an apologetic introduction to a modem letter.[43]

Even Dibelius, who accepted the 95–96 date, found the words, *συμφοράς* and *περιπτώσεις*, "mild expressions."[44]

Welborn rightly asks, "Is the phrase, *συμφορὰς καὶ περιπτώσεις*, susceptible of the strong reading which scholars customarily give it?"[45] In fact, these words, taken out of their context in 1 Clement (and it is precisely that context which we should try to determine!), are much less sensational and negative than they appear, say, in Lake's translation cited above: "misfortunes and calamities." Welborn shows that in Attic Greek *συμφορα* often means nothing more than "event" or "circumstance." Its colorlessness is apparent in a proverb of Herodotus: "Events rule men, not men events" (*αἱ συμφοραὶ τῶν ἀνθρώπων ἄρχουσι καὶ ουχὶ ὤνθρωποι τῶν συμφορέων*).[46] Early writers must add a qualifying word to give it a negative meaning.

Thus Herodotus speaks of *συμφορὴ ἄχαρις*[47] *ανδ Αεσξηψλυσ οφ κακὴ συμφορά*.[48] Welborn could have strengthened this point by referring to the two times in which the cognate *σύμφορος* is used in the New Testament: in 1 Corinthians 7:35: "I say this for your own benefit (*σύμφορον*)", and 1 Corinthians 10:33, "... not seeking my own advantage (*σύμφορον*)." The least that can be said is that the word does not usually have a negative meaning.

The case is similar with *περίπτωσις*. Welborn shows that it means "experience" or "accident" rather than "calamity." Sextus epitomizes his empirical philosophy in the dictum, "All understanding is the result of experience (*πᾶσα νόησις γίνεται ἀπὸ περιπτώσεως*)."[49]

Thus, Welborn's linguistic examination of 1:1 calls into real question whether anything like a persecution was meant by the text at all.[50]

43 E. T. Merrill, "The Alleged Persecution by Domitian," in *Essays in Early Christian History*, 160.

44 M[artin] Dibelius, *Botschaft and Geschichte II*, 192.

45 Welborn, *op. cit.*, 38.

46 Herodotus, 7:49; cf. 1:32.

47 Ibid., 1:41.

48 Aeschylus, *Persae*, 445.

49 Sextus, *SVF II*, 22,29.

50 Welborn cites impressive authority for the thesis that Domitian did not persecute the Christians: E. T. Merrill, *Essays in Early Christian History*, 148–173; R. L. P. Milburn, "The Persecution of Domitian," in *CQR* 139 (1945): 154–64; R. M. Grant, *Augustus to Constantine*, 1970, 79–80; G. E.

But even if some persecution or adversity were meant, one is still obliged to determine if it is accurate to assign Domitian as the cause of the trouble. Again, this issue of whether or not Domitian was involved is crucial since so much depends upon linking the events spoken of in 1 Clement to his reign, the dates of which are considered certain. Likewise, it is Eusebius, not the text of 1 Clement, who mentions Domitian by name. As long as authors commenting on 1 Clement were satisfied that some adversity or persecution was meant by 1:1, they saw this as corroborative of Eusebius' information that Clemens was bishop of Rome toward the end of Domitian's reign, and that very probably, then, 1:1 referred to his persecution.

If, though, we argue independently of Eusebius, and ask whether Domitian can be said to have ever persecuted the Church at all, in and of itself a negative answer will not determine a date for 1 Clement, but, *via negativa*, will show just how weak the AD 95–96 dating hypothesis really is. That is our immediate purpose here.

During Domitian's reign, two great Roman historians flourished: Suetonius and Dio Cassius.[51] Each of them record valuable information about the Roman emperors of and before their time. Neither mentions any persecution of the Christians. Welborn, again following Merrill, finds this silence noteworthy since Suetonius had recorded among Nero's praiseworthy deeds that he put to death Christians, "*genus hominum superstitionis novae ac malificae.*" Welborn argues that, had Suetonius known of Domitian's persecution, he would doubtless have mentioned it.[52]

Having traced the earliest reference to a persecution under Domitian to Melito of Sardis, who in circa AD 170–180 had merely accused Domitian of bringing "false accusations" against Christians, Welborn goes on to show that the first explicit allegation against Domitian to this effect comes in Tertullian's *Apology*:

> Nero was the first who assailed the Christian sect with the imperial sword. Domitian, too, a man of Nero's type in cruelty, attempted the same things; but he had something of the human in him, and soon put an end to what he had begun, even restoring those whom he had banished.[53]

Says Welborn, "the source of Tertullian's statement is unknown, but it is likely that it rests upon nothing more than Melito and his own imagination. ... His statement that Domitian himself restored the exiles is incorrect; their recall took

---

M. de Ste. Croix, "Why Were the Early Christians Persecuted?" *Past and Present* 26 (1963): 15, and A.Y. Collins, *Crisis and Catharsis*, 54–83.

51 Suetonius, *Domitianus*; Dio Cassius, 67.

52 Welborn, *op. cit.*, 40.

53 Tertullian, *Apol.* no. 5; Welborn, *op. cit.*, 41.

place under Nerva. Tertullian makes no secret of the apologetic principles which have shaped his vision of history: only the wicked persecuted Christians."[54]

It would follow that, having persecuted the Christians, Nero and Domitian were merely behaving according to their wicked nature, a judgement Tertullian would have shared with public opinion since they were the only two emperors to suffer the notorious *post mortem damnatio memoriae*. Thus, investigation shows that evidence for any persecution under Domitian is itself weak. This would strengthen Welborn's previous contention that persecution is not even suggested by the very text of 1:1.

To what then does it refer?

Welborn goes on to develop an elaborate thesis that the phrase "*συμφορὰς καὶ περιπτώσεις*" refers to "internal dissensions like those that troubled the community at Corinth. But it is not necessary to believe that these quarrels had any real existence at all, only that the author found allusion to them, by means of conventional expressions, a convenient way of establishing a sympathetic relationship between himself and his readers. He wished to say: "we are faced with the same problems and have need of the same admonition."[55]

In other words, Welborn suggests that 1:1 is a *captatio benevolentiae*, an attempt on 1 Clement's part to gain a hearing from the Corinthians since he shows his understanding of their situation.

One of the motives for Welborn choosing to interpret 1:1 as rhetorical was perhaps his distrust of seeing in the phrase any precise historical events. Having shown that it did not refer to a persecution under Domitian, Welborn was content not to have to explain what it referred to except to say that it fitted the rhetoric of 1 Clement's argument. His hesitation is understandable. Still, there is another hypothesis, one that Welborn does not mention, and that is, if 1 Clement were understood to have been written in AD 70 instead of AD 96, perhaps the words of 1:1 might refer, not to internal strife, but to something that had happened recently in Roman society. It was Edmundson in 1913, who, recognizing the weakness of the Domitian-persecution hypothesis, entertained the idea that 1 Clement might be dated in circa AD 70 and that 1 Clement 1:1 might instead refer to the chaotic

---

54 Welborn, *op. cit.*, 41. It is nevertheless worthy of note that practically all the commentaries on the New Testament, when discussing the date of the Apocalypse, do seem to assert that there *was* a persecution under Domitian, and then proceed to date the Apocalypse to his reign. This is problematic enough for the reasons here stated, but strictly speaking, even if there *had* been a persecution under Domitian, one would still have to show that *Domitian's* persecution is being referred to in 1 Clement 1:1. Cf. W. G. Kummel, *Introduction to the New Testament*, 466–469. Interesting here is W. H. C. Frend who, in *Martyrdom and Persecution in the Early Church*, 160–161, argues *from* 1 Clement *against* a Domitianic persecution: "The remainder of the letter gives no hint that anything had been amiss with the Christians at Rome. Praise for the Roman legionaries (ch. 37) would have read like misplaced humour if in fact the Church in Rome had just been suffering repressive measures."

55 Ibid., 48.

political situation in Rome during the year 69. He quotes Philostratus' *Life of Apollonius of Tyana* for the impact of the repeated upheavals of that year:

> Galba was killed at Rome itself after grasping at the Empire; Otho, killed in lower Gaul, was not even buried with honor, but lies like a common man. And destiny flew through all this history in one year.[56]

The year of the so-called "Barracks Emperors" must have been a difficult one indeed, especially for the population of the capital. What makes this explanation additionally attractive is that it fits nicely with the translation of "*συμφορὰς καὶ περιπτώσεις*" as events and happenings which were sudden and repeated. It explains why 1 Clement could be so vague: the whole Empire surely knew what had so recently occurred. First Clement's plan of sending church emissaries to Corinth could easily have had to be postponed with the predictable chaos at the ports. Only when Vespasian succeeded Vitellius did there seem to be a return to civil peace.

Obviously, such a reference would be hard to prove. It suffices for our purposes to note, in summary, that the traditional interpretation of 1:1 has to be abandoned, i.e., that it is a reference to a persecution of the Church under the Emperor Domitian. Thus, the link between 1 Clement and the circa AD 96 dating is further weakened. At the very least it can be said that a circa AD 70 dating is by no means precluded by 1 Clement 1:1.

Closely linked to the question of whether 1 Clement 1 has anything to do with persecution is the reference in 1 Clement 7:1:

> We are not only writing these things to you, beloved, for your admonition, but also to remind ourselves; for we are in the same arena (ἐν γὰρ τῷ αὐτῷ ἐσμὲν σκάμματι) and the same struggle is before us (*ὁ αὐτὸς ἡμῖν ἀγὼν ἐπίκειται*)

Our first consideration would be, what are "these things" that Clement has just written and which he now says can also apply to his own situation? It is true that in chapter 5, he mentions Peter and Paul and the fact that they were persecuted to death. Then, in chapter 6, he mentions others who were persecuted in the violent, physical sense of the word. Thus, it is not surprising that some commentators have thought that the alleged persecution motif continues into chapter 7 and thus 1 Clement repeats here that he is writing at a time of persecution. From that point, it took little to add the traditional information that 1 Clement was bishop of Rome toward the end of the reign of Domitian, and thus must be referring to that Emperor's persecution of the Church. While the weak grounds upon which one

---

56 In *Apol.* 5.13 (tr. Phillimore, II, 58); 4 in Edmundson, *op. cit.*, 191. Referred to in Robinson, *op. cit.*, 329. See also A. E. Wilhelm-Hooijbergh, *op. cit.*, 267. For an overall view of the situation in the Empire in AD 69, see K. Wellesley, *The Long Year*, AD 69, *passim*.

speaks of a formal persecution against the Church under Domitian have already been treated, one might rightly ask whether we have here in 7:1 a counter-indication that in fact there may have been a persecution after all.

To rebut this argument, it is first of all essential to see that 1 Clement is not writing to console the Corinthians during a time of persecution. His clear purpose in using the horrible examples of chapters 5 and 6 was to condemn, not persecution, but jealousy and envy, which, he says, were behind the persecutions in the first place. In other words he uses the persecutions as examples of jealousy, thus marking them as clearly wrong and from which repentance is needed as he continues in chapters 7 and 8:

> 7:5: Let us review all the generations and let us learn that ... the Master has given a place of repentance to those who will turn to him.
>
> 8:1ff.: The ministers of the grace of God spoke through the Holy Spirit concerning repentance , etc.

Therefore, our verse 7:1 is located in a transition from examples of jealousy to a call for repentance. This is just as we should have thought since this is precisely 1 Clement's main purpose, to get the Corinthians to repent of their ouster of their presbyters which 1 Clement attributes to jealousy.

It can therefore be seen that the mention of persecution was only secondary to 1 Clement's main point against jealousy. I would maintain then, that when he says that we are in the same situation, 1 Clement means to allude to the fact that, as presbyters in Rome, they realize what it is like to be the victims of jealousy.

Three points in the text should be examined.

The first is 1 Clement's use of σκάμμα or arena. It is true that it refers to the athletic arena, but its first meaning is "that which has been dug", and so can mean a trench for water, a grave, or the dug up and sanded pit in which athletes competed. Clearly, though, 1 Clement uses the word as a kind of metaphor and prepares us for the ἀγών, or "struggle" which follows. The word has been used with a variety of metaphorical applications but since 1 Clement is not speaking *ex professo* about persecutions but jealousy, there seems little to warrant the supposition that σκάμμα should be taken to refer to the arena in which some of the persecutions undoubtedly took place.

The word ἀγών means struggle and likewise *could* be used metaphorically to refer to the struggle undergone by those who suffered persecution, but not necessarily. We should note that 1 Clement says of both σκάμμα and ἀγών that they are αὐτός, the same. The same, it is clear, as the arena and the struggle of the Corinthians. There is not the slightest hint that the Corinthians are undergoing state persecution; so the metaphor refers, it seems, to the internal struggle over the presbyters which, we have seen, 1 Clement has already likened to the jealousy which sparked the persecutions of the just in the past.

It is reasonable to conclude that 1 Clement is saying that the presbyters of Rome share the struggles of the Corinthian Church. Those struggles have to do with the problems of jealousy which seem to occur frequently. Any reference to state persecution is so remote as to seem most unlikely here.

1.3 "Those appointed by the Apostles ... and for many years" (1 Clement 44:3)

44:3 is also relevant to our study of the dating of 1 Clement:

> We consider (*νομίζομεν*) therefore that it is not just to remove (*ἀποβάλλεσθαι*) from their ministry those who were appointed by them (the apostles), or later on by other eminent men ... and have ministered ... and for many years have received a universally favorable testimony.

It could be argued that the phrase "*νομίζομεν ἀποβάλλεσθαι* " is grammatically ambiguous: with both the main verb and the infinitive in the present tense, the sense could be that "we think that it would (always) be wrong to oust." The grammatical ambiguity is resolved however by the context: there is never any mention by 1 Clement that apostolic appointees had ever previously been expelled. Therefore, his probable meaning is that it would be wrong for the Corinthians to do so *now*, i.e. at the time of the writing.

There are basically two issues here: first that some of the presbyters ousted by the Corinthians were themselves appointed by the Apostles and second, that the ousted presbyters had served "for many years."

The first point, in addition to being important to our specific study, has a wider theological significance which should not go unnoticed here. First, Clement is stating directly and as part of his argument to the Corinthians that there were some of the ousted presbyters who were appointed by the Apostles, presumably by either Peter or Paul, the only Apostles known by name to 1 Clement and who both had close ties with the community, as we know from 1 Corinthians. What is not generally recognized, is that this assertion is in the context of an adamant, if risky, insistence on the part of 1 Clement that the Corinthians do what must have been very embarrassing for them to do, namely to reinstate the presbyters who had been ejected. Those who claim that the Apostles appointed no one and that such apostolic appointment is a fiction of a later era, imply that 1) 1 Clement did not mean what he said (though if it were not common knowledge that they *had* been appointed by the Apostles, his whole argument is severely jeopardized) and 2) that 1 Clement did not presume that he could rely on the Corinthians' memory of the origin of this practice of the Apostles' appointing presbyters. It seems very far fetched to think that 1 Clement would take the risk of making a new and groundless assertion. It seems much more reasonable to acknowledge that we have here a clear statement that the Apostles did in fact appoint presbyters since this assertion forms such a central part of 1 Clement's argument.[57]

Presuming, then, that the Apostles *did* appoint presbyters, which is not an uncontested presumption as we shall see later, we still have to ask when they might have done this. The point is important since 44:3 apparently implies that some of these appointees have survived until the time of the writing of 1 Clement. On the premise that it does so, how can this help determine the most probable date of 1 Clement?

Although we have the two canonical letters of Paul to the Corinthians, they too are undated and we have no way of telling when Peter or Paul may last have been in Corinth. Still, it was probably substantially before their deaths in circa 67 since there is general agreement that they died after some period of continual residence in the city. If we say that they were probably not to return to Corinth after 62 (though perhaps long before), we have a kind of *terminus ante quem* for the appointing of these presbyters. If we then think of the AD 96 date, we have to think of these presbyters as surviving, at least some of them, for some 35 years *as presbyters*.

At this point one might be tempted to resort to some kind of argument about the average age expectancy in the ancient world, but that approach is unsound both because of the fact that it is really no more than a modern educated guess, and because even if we can determine an average age expectancy, there would be nothing to show that certain individuals had not exceeded that average. Perhaps it would be better to reflect upon the identity of a presbyter in the early church. There may be a clue to its meaning which endures in the basic denotation of the word. Πρεσβύτερος is the comparative degree of the adjective πρέσβυς and is used almost always substantively: an *elder*. A natural question immediately arises, "Elder than whom?" Of course it means "elder" as regards the rest of the community. As exercising some function within the community, the elder is first and foremost himself a member of the community.

The term is quite common in Judaism prior to and during the New Testament period. In Acts, for example, it is used seven times referring to the group of elders who, with the high priests, Luke considers to be the leaders of the Jews. It is used ten times to refer to an analogous group in the nascent Christian community, with the Apostles taking the place of the high priests. It is interesting to note that it is

57 See R. Brown and J. Meier, *Antioch and Rome*, 175: "... we must remember Clement has to persuade the Corinthians who received his letter: surely, they would have recognized and rejected a pure fabrication about the origins of the presbyterate. The solution that seems most plausible is that 1 Clement has generalized an apostolic practice that was occasional but not consistent or universal."

always used in the plural in Acts, suggesting some collegial or corporate method of government. The term is very common in the Synoptics to refer to leaders of the Jews. Even 1 Clement reflects this: "The blessed Judith, when her city was besieged, asked the elders to suffer her to go." (54:4). The term is absent from the Pauline corpus, appearing only in the Pastorals. Paul does, however, speak of a kind of "elder", without using the precise term, when he refers in 1 Corinthians 16:15 to the household of Stephanas the "first fruits" of Achaia, i.e. one of his first converts there. They have "appointed themselves for the service of the saints." Paul urges the Corinthians to be "subject to such men."

Says J.H. Elliott:

> The Corinthians were to subordinate themselves to Stephanas and his household because these people were, as the first converts, "seniors in the faith." They were elders, as it were, not necessarily in natural age but in Christian experience and service.[58]

And again,

> It is possible, perhaps probable, that when they (the Christians) chose and designated their leaders as "elders" the criterion for this choice was not merely natural age, but the length of age as a Christian, seniority in the faith.[59]

We shall refer to the usage in the Pastorals below, but for now it seems preferable to keep the other New Testament references to πρεσβύτεροι separate because of the dating issue: the remaining books most probably date from the period after AD 70 and hence are irrelevant to establish a possible pre-70 Christian understanding of the term. The Gospels and Acts reflect at least the widespread Jewish usage of the term, and the presence of that term in the oral tradition prior to the Gospels' composition.

Naturally, even if the Stephanas passage does reflect the origin of the term "elder" in the sense of one tried in the faith for a lengthy period of time, it was not long before the first converts had passed away, and so the office gradually came to be linked not to the original converts but those who had proven themselves. Keeping in mind also the fact that the community did not need *many* such leaders, it is only logical that some criteria should gradually be developed whereby the elder could be selected from the community members at large.[60] In any case, what concerns us here is not *what* those criteria were, but *that* some discretionary

58 J. H. Elliott, *A Home for the Homeless*, 190.

59 Ibid., 191.

60 Cf. Brown and Meier, *op. cit.*, 163, no. 348. In discussing the similar transition from a presbyteral college to monepiscopacy, Brown makes this commonsense and valuable comment: "No magical one moment for the introduction of the single-bishop is in mind. The line of demarcation was

principles had to be developed other than mere natural age. It would also follow that someone would have to do the selecting. It is curious that 1 Corinthians 16:15 says explicitly that it was the household of Stephanas who "appointed themselves" (ἔταξαν ἑαυτούς). But Paul shows no difficulty with this method of selection and confirms it: "you should be subject to such men." It may be, then, that leadership in the early community developed naturally or spontaneously enough, at least from the social point of view. Still, we do have Paul himself seemingly designating a group of people as leaders in the Corinthian community. All of this is mentioned to lay to rest the often implicit objection that Paul, because he did not use the term πρεσβύτερος, did not know of the function of elder.

Continuing to hypothesize that he actually *did* appoint presbyters, do the facts, as well as we can determine them, allow us to reconcile 1 Clement 44:3 with a date of composition in the mid-90's? The issues are these:

1. some of the apostolic appointees are still alive,
2. a second "generation" of presbyters, appointed "by other eminent men," overlaps with the original group,
3. and this situation has gone on "for many years."

The central problem, it seems, is whether "many years" refers to all or just some of the elders in question. If one recognizes that the fact that the ousted elders have served many years with universally favorable testimony forms part of 1 Clement's rhetorical argument, then we would not necessarily be obliged to think that *all* of the ousted elders had done so, but perhaps only the original ones. First Clement is trying to bring moral pressure upon the Corinthians to reinstate the elders. He describes them as a mixed group, some of whom were appointed by the Apostles, some not. He is trying to argue that there are no grounds, no justifiable grounds at least, for the Corinthians' action. The fact that the presbyteral structure has been functioning for many years is simply further proof of the illegitimacy of the ouster. Therefore, while 1 Clement 44:3, in itself does not argue for an AD 70 dating, it has nothing against it. However, it does seem to discourage a later date because of the probable continued survival of some apostolic appointees.

1.4 "Those nearest to us, of our own generation" (1 Clement 5)

The next section we should examine is the whole of chapter 5.

> But to cease from the examples of old time, let us come to those who contended in the days nearest (ἔγγιστα) to us; let us

surely fuzzy between the fully acknowledged single-bishop and the *de facto* prominence of one of the presbyter-bishops by force of personality, brains, wealth, etc."

> take the noble examples of our own generation (τῆς γενεᾶς ἡμῶν). Through jealousy and envy the greatest and most righteous pillars of the Church were persecuted and contended unto death. Let us set before our eyes the good apostles: Peter, who because of unrighteous jealousy suffered not one or two but many trials, and having thus given his testimony, went to the glorious place which was his due. Through jealousy and strife, Paul showed the way to the prize of endurance; seven times he was in bonds, he was exiled, he was stoned, he was a herald both in the East and in the West, he gained the noble fame of his faith, he taught righteousness to all the world, and when he had reached the limits of the West he gave his testimony before the rulers, and thus passed from the world and was taken up into the Holy Place—the greatest example of endurance.

This passage is relevant to the dating question in several ways. They will be treated in the order of their occurrence in the text. First, there is a very important, but universally overlooked question inherent in the use of the superlative ἔγγιστα in 5:1: "in the days nearest to us." In the Greek, ἔγγιστα is actually an adverbial accusative: ἐπὶ τοὺς ἔγγιστα γενομένους ἀθλητάς. What is to be noted in particular is that the adverb is superlative where one might have expected the simple or the comparative degree, since the whole point is a transition from ancient examples of jealousy cited in chapter 4, to non-ancient, i.e. "close" or "closer" examples of the same nature as the deaths of the Apostles. The comparative contrast (and *not* the superlative) is only heightened by the fact that the ancient examples in chapter 4 are all taken from Scripture (introduced in 4:1, Γέγραπται γὰρ οὕτως), while the ones cited as *nearest* are not.

The superlative in English is translated either by *nearest, very near,* or *as near as possible.* One can only ask then, is it reasonable that 1 Clement, writing in the middle nineties, would still think of the Apostles' deaths thirty years before as "very near"? One should keep in mind that the entire Christian movement would have been only circa 70 years old by the mid-nineties. Secondly, the question is made precise by 1 Clement's addition of the phrase, "of our own generation."

Jaubert recognized that the term could imply that the author had been alive at the time of the Neronian persecution.[61] But 1 Clement says pointedly "our" generation, not meaning simply his own, but in the context of the lesson he is trying to teach to his Corinthian readers, *their* generation as well.

If one were to compare 1 Clement's understanding of "generation" as he himself uses it in 11:3, the sense is perhaps more clear. Having referred in the beginning of the verse to the punishment of Lot's wife who "became a pillar of salt to this day,"

61 Jaubert, *Epître aux Corinthiens*, 19.

1 Clement contends that this was done "to make known to all that those who are double-minded and have doubts concerning the power of God, incur judgement and become a warning to all *generations*." He is implying, by the very use of the example of Lot's wife, her disobedience and her punishment, that his Corinthian readers likewise risk punishment for their disobedience. His quaint assertion that the very pillar of salt is still somewhere to be seen is to imply that she is a warning to the present generation, as she has been to those past. In other words, she is a warning to the Corinthians, the addressees of 1 Clement. Obviously if both 1 Clement and his readers belong to the same generation as Peter and Paul, it seems clear that he is not referring to a past period so far back that a large number of his readers would not even have been alive, as would be the case by the mid 90's.

Again, the dating of the mid-nineties is the problem. The date of circa 70 poses no such difficulties.

In his rejection of a date earlier than "75-80 AD," Lake says of 1 Clement: "It appears from chapter 5 to be later than the persecution of Nero and from chaps. 42-44 that the age of the apostles is regarded as past."[62]

We turn now to a consideration of what 1 Clement meant by *apostle*.

It is striking that 1 Clement calls both Peter and Paul Apostles. By that very fact he sets himself apart from the simple "12 apostles" tradition of the Synoptics and much closer to the Pauline usage.[63] In fact 1 Clement shows no knowledge of the apostleship being limited at any time to the Twelve. He calls Paul an Apostle again in 47:1: "Take up the epistle of the blessed Paul the Apostle," echoing the insistence of Paul in 1 Corinthians that he was indeed an Apostle (1 Corinthians 1:1; 4:9; 9:1, 2; 15:9).[64]

---

62 K. Lake, *op. cit.*, 4.

63 The issue of the distinction between the "Twelve", the "disciples" and the "Apostles" is notoriously difficult and not much appreciated before the modern era. Apparently it was J. B. Lightfoot who first alluded to the question in his 1865 commentary on the Galatians. For a general overview of the scholarly efforts to explain the developments and distinctions within the Apostolic age, see W. Schmitals, *The Office of Apostle in the Early Church*. It must be admitted, of course, that in itself the term *genea* is rather broad. It can even be used to mean something like "lifetime", as for example in Irenaeus V, 30, 3 (commenting on the Apocalypse): "For that was seen no very long time ago but almost in our own day, (*schedon epi tēs hēmeteras geneas*) toward the end of Domitian's reign." (Irenaeus AH 5.30.3)

It should be noticed, though, that Ireneaus's point was to emphasize the shortness of time (which could have been almost eighty years) between when he wrote and the death of Domitian. The effort then was to lengthen the term *genea* so as practically to include Domitian. Also, Irenaeus does not use the superlative (as in *engista*) but the simple form of *schedon*.

Summing up this point, it seems that 1 Clement's language would emphasize the shortness of time between when he wrote and the lifetimes of the Apostles. While we do not have here anything so precise as a *dating* reference, it can be plausibly argued that the time of the Apostles is not envisioned as long before.

64 Since it is clear that 1 Clement is familiar with the canonical 1 Corinthians, it could be supposed

While it is true that the Synoptics do not count anyone else but the Twelve as being Apostles, it is also true that their time-line is the earthly life and the immediate post-resurrection period, and hence they do not treat of other Apostles *ex professo*. Acts 14:14 does call Paul and Barnabas Apostles: "But when the Apostles Barnabas and Paul heard of it, they tore their garments." And again in 14:4: "but the people in the city were divided: some sided with the Jews, some with the Apostles (Paul and Barnabas)."

On the other hand, it has to be admitted that these passages contradict others in Acts where Paul is constantly interacting with the Apostles, not as a peer, but as a non-Apostle: 9:27: "But Barnabas took him (Saul) and brought him to the Apostles"; 15:2: "Paul and Barnabas were appointed to go up to Jerusalem to the Apostles and the elders about this question"; 15:4 "When they (Paul and Barnabas) came to Jerusalem, they were welcomed by the Apostles and the elders"; 16:6: "As they (Paul and Timothy) went through the cities they delivered ... the decisions which had been reached by the Apostles and elders in Jerusalem." It seems that while Luke knows of the tradition of Paul being an Apostle, he is generally "downgraded" as not being one of the Jerusalem Apostles who formed a kind of standing committee for church affairs. This Lukan portrait of the Twelve, all of whom were Apostles (so much so that when they become the Eleven, Matthias has to be chosen to complete the number), with some recognition of the apostleship of Paul, seems to be a later development.

There is no question that Paul in the introduction to the Romans and the Galatians is defending himself against charges that he was not truly an Apostle: "an Apostle, not from men nor through man, but through Jesus Christ and God the Father" (Galatians 1:1). The standard hypothesis is that the notion of the 12 Apostles developed as a kind of counter-balance to the very successful Pauline mission. Whatever the case, 1 Clement is entirely innocent of the conflict: he in fact knows only two Apostles, Peter and Paul, by name.[65] It is true that in 44 1 Clement does seem to know of a larger group of Apostles:

---

that he is therefore aware of the "twelve apostles" tradition via 1 Corinthians 15:5 where Paul speaks of Christ appearing to "the Twelve". But Paul does not say "twelve *apostles*". In fact, he distinguishes another apparition in which Christ appears to "James, then to all the apostles", suggesting that Paul consistently resisted an equation between the "twelve" and the "apostles". He at least would have insisted that there were thirteen, in order to include himself! See W. Schmitals, *op. cit.*, 88: "Paul is not aware of any group of twelve 'apostles' at all." See also G. Sass, "Der Apostel in der Didache" in *In Memoriam E. Lohmeyer*, 1951, 12: "Before Paul and at the time of Paul ... the group of the twelve did not qualify as apostles."

65 Nevertheless, the presumption that 1 Clement knows of a *twelve* Apostles tradition is common. Cf. Schmitals, *op. cit*, 266; more surprisingly, R. Brown, *The Churches the Apostles Left Behind*, 16f, "The classical answer, already given in 1 Clement (42 and 44), is that just as Jesus appointed apostles (understood to be the Twelve along with Paul), so also the apostles appointed bishops or presbyters to succeed them."

> Our apostles also knew through our Lord Jesus Christ that there would be strife for the title of bishop. For this reason, therefore, since they had received perfect foreknowledge, they appointed those who have already been mentioned.

It seems improbable that 1 Clement, whenever he wrote, knew of *only* two Apostles. Nevertheless, he cannot be said to know of the fully developed Synoptic tradition of the Twelve, complete with names. In response, then, to Lake, cited above, not only does 1 Clement seem not to reflect a time when the Apostolic period had passed, the Synoptic Gospels may not have even yet been written![66]

The general relationship of 1 Clement to the New Testament will be discussed at a further point, but to summarize the significance of this individual passage for the dating issue, one might say that it seems to reflect a time period much closer to the actual deaths of the Apostles Peter and Paul than the mid-nineties hypothesis. The fact that 1 Clement knows nothing of the 12 Apostle tradition would tend to locate 1 Clement before the development of that tradition in the Synoptics or at least prior to the circulation of the Synoptic Gospels and thus considerably earlier than AD 96.

1.5 "Even then you made yourselves partisans" (1 Clement 47:3)

Though not discussed in this connection by other commentators on 1 Clement, this verse may have some value for the question of dating because of its direct rhetorical force of accusation. The context is 1 Clement's appeal to the teaching of Paul in 1 Corinthians. He has told his readers in 47:1: "Take up the epistle of blessed Paul the Apostle. What did he first write to you at the beginning of his preaching? With true inspiration he charged you concerning himself and Cephas and Apollos, because even then you made yourselves partisans." In 1 Corinthians Paul delivered an impassioned plea against factionalism which threatened to divide the community into parties devoted to Peter, Paul or Apollos. First Clement's reference to that chastisement which the Corinthians had received from Paul would have been blunt enough to a community whose forebears had received it, but 1 Clement is even more severe: "you made yourselves partisans." He does not say "your fathers made themselves partisans" or "in the past factionalism took hold of the Corinthian Church," but actually charges that his readers, "you" were responsible. That 1 Clement saw the severity of this can be shown from the following verse where he softens the blow by conceding, "But that partisanship entailed less guilt on you: for you were the partisans of Apostles, and of a man approved by them."

Would such bluntness be excessive if addressed to a community whose members had been responsible for divisiveness some 30–50 years before, (presuming

66 Contra, Brown, *Antioch and Rome*, 159, "... in chaps. 42 and 44 he (1 Clement) speaks of the apostles as a past generation."

that 1 Clement was written in AD 96). The easier answer is: yes, it would. Again, one has to return to the situation in which 1 Clement finds himself: he is asking the Corinthians to reinstate presbyters and is sending them emissaries to underscore the seriousness of his intervention. Surely the Corinthians would be embarrassed and even resentful of 1 Clement's intervention. In such a climate, would 1 Clement risk alienating his readers unnecessarily by accusing them of something that *they themselves* were not guilty of, i.e. past factionalism? First Clement's task was delicate enough without the gratuitously offensive "you."

On the other hand, if the epistle were written in AD 70, the situation is entirely different. We have already seen that some of Paul's own appointees have survived until 1 Clement's time. If indeed the same individuals who caused Paul problems were acting up again, 1 Clement's "you" is not offensive but factual. This would make all the more logical the citation from 1 Corinthians in the first place since the very people whom Paul corrected had not yet learned their lesson.

1.6 "... the ancient Church of the Corinthians" (1 Clement 47:6)

The basic issue is plain enough: if 1 Clement calls the Corinthian Church "ancient" (ἀρχαίαν) how old does it have to be?

It will be noticed that this text follows immediately upon the previous one in which 1 Clement appeals to 1 Corinthians which he says Paul wrote to the Corinthians ἐν ἀρχῇ τοῦ εὐαγγελίου. Says Robinson:

> ... evidently in the context the meaning of ἀρχαίαν is determined by the phrase "the ἀρχή of the Gospel," which is precisely that used by Paul to the Philippians of the period when he first preached to them—after an interval of only a decade (Phil. 4,15; see also Luke 1:2; Acts 11:15; 1 John 2:7, 24; 3:11; 2 John 6). Similarly, in Acts 15:7 ἀφ' ἡμέρων ἀρχαίων is used at the Council of Jerusalem of "the early days" less than twenty years previously, and Manson, "a Christian from the early days" is described already by Luke in the early 60s as an ἀρχαῖος μαθητής (Acts 21:16)."[67]

Without entering into Robinson's whole view of the dating of Acts, he seems to make the point clearly enough that ἀρχαῖος is at best a relative term. The Corinthian Church is ἀρχαία not simply because of the passage of time, but because it is old when compared to more recently established communities. It may also be seen as old when one recalls that the entire Christian movement is not all that ancient itself, whether it is circa 65 years old if 1 Clement is written in the mid-

67 Robinson, *op. cit.*, 332.

nineties, or whether it is only 40 years old in AD 70. In the latter hypothesis, the Corinthian Church could be 25.[68] Perhaps in absolute numbers 25 may not appear much when compared to two millenia of Church history today. But it seems quite appropriate to speak of a community as ἀρχαία if it were more than half as old as the entire Christian movement.

In any case, it does not appear that a date of AD 70 is ruled out by 1 Clement's referring to the Corinthians' Church as ἀρχαία.

1.7 "... who have lived among us from youth to old age" (1 Clement 63:3)

There are three distinct but related issues which remain to be considered within the text of 1 Clement itself. All three have to do with the fact that 1 Clement is sending, along with the letter itself, three representatives.

This matter of sending three representatives has not been given the attention it deserves in the examination of whether 1 Clement constitutes an early "papal" intervention. It is known that Paul often sent trusted individuals to his various churches. First Clement in adopting this Pauline (though hardly exclusively so) practice is adding considerable clout to his exhortation contained in the letter. Though their "legal" identity or actual jurisdiction was probably not defined especially among the faction who were being chastened by 1 Clement, the three representatives sent with a strong written correction, appear to be "enforcers." They can avoid the endless delays generated by the great distance which lay between Rome and Corinth. The revolutionaries, if their actual identities were unknown to 1 Clement, would be discovered immediately. The real reaction of the community would be witnessed first hand and reported back to 1 Clement. It is not possible for us to know what 1 Clement would or could have done had his plea been ignored, but the very sending of these emissaries also suggests that he thought his chances of winning were quite good. What the immediate effect of the mission was, however, we shall never know. We can tell both historically and from the fact that the letter is later held in such great reverence in Corinth that the community did return to the presbyteral structure, but with what travail? Were other measures necessary? We have no way of telling.

Suffice it to say, however, that this act that 1 Clement sent three representatives was no minor detail: it underscores the seriousness of the entire affair. When they are first mentioned, in 63:3, 1 Clement says: "We have sent faithful and prudent men who have lived among us from youth to old age." Briefly, the question which concerns us here is whether, in AD 70, it could have been possible for these men to have lived "from youth to old age" and "among us."

68 The obvious, implicit, and perhaps unanswerable question is, when did Christianity arrive in Corinth? For a fuller discussion see Murphy-O'Connor, *op. cit.*, *passim*, but esp. 140, "Paul could not have reached Corinth before A.D. 45."

Lightfoot addressed this question directly and judged against any date earlier than AD 95–96:

> If the epistle was written about AD 68 or earlier, how could it be said of any Roman Christian that he had lived from youth to old age in the Church of Christ, seeing that the first Apostle visited Rome about AD 60, and that two years earlier when writing to the Roman Church, while recognizing the existence of a Christian Congregation, he speaks throughout as though this were practically virgin soil in which he was called to sow the seed of the Gospel?[69]

Several issues have to be raised here, however. The first is whether, when 1 Clement says "among us," he is really referring to the Christian community *per se*, or whether he means that among the Christians of Rome these individuals are known to have been men of high character, irrespective of when they became Christians. In other words, "us" could mean simply that they were known in Rome, not necessarily just within the Church.

Robinson goes further and notes that it is not impossible that they were Christians for a considerable time. He points to Acts 2:10 which refers to converts from Rome being present at Pentecost, and in Romans 16:6ff., Paul greets Andronicus and Junias as eminent among the Apostles adding, "They were Christians before I was."[70]

In addition, it is not at all clear that Romans was written to a community which Paul considered neophyte. From one point of view, Romans can be seen as a rather sophisticated theological treatise intended to "introduce" Paul to the Roman community, thus suggesting they were the opposite of "virgin soil."[71]

Lightfoot suffers, as well, from a too absolute view of the meaning of "old age": "Old age could hardly be predicated of persons under sixty."[72] This may have been a matter of course for English usage in the 1870's, but when one considers that the average age expectancy in the first century was considerably lower than 60, "old age" could mean nothing more than, perhaps 50, or even more broadly, it may refer to what we would call adulthood, or maturity. The presupposition that the delegates were in their sixties when 1 Clement was written also requires us to believe that these old men were being sent on a journey probably of some weeks duration, and which was bound to be quite grueling even from a psychological standpoint. There is nothing objective in the text, or in what we know otherwise

69 Lightfoot, *op. cit.*, 349.

70 Robinson, *op. cit.*, 331.

71 I refer here, of course, to the long-standing debate over the exact genre of the Romans; see esp. *The Romans Debate*, ed. Karl P. Donfried.

72 Lightfoot, *op. cit.*, 27.

of the first century, to demand that these delegates be as old as sixty, or that they had to have lived all of that time as Christians. In other words, not only does this reference not exclude a date in circa AD 70, it makes it very improbable that very old men would have been sent at all, making the later dating unnecessary.

1.8 "... Claudius Ephebus and Valerius Vito" (1 Clement 65:1)

The next issue we should examine is the actual names of the first two delegates, Claudius Ephebus and Valerius Vito. Lightfoot saw here a probable reference to two *liberti*, manumitted slaves of the Emperor Claudius and of his wife Valeria.[73] This is an interesting possibility, but several facts have to be considered.

Claudius succeeded Tiberius in AD 41 and reigned until AD 54.[74] It is possible that in his will Claudius provided for the manumission of Ephebus, who took the Emperor's name as his *praenomen*.[75] If we presume that Ephebus was thirty in AD 54 (he could have been older, or younger, though the freed slave to become a Roman *civis* had to be at least thirty at the time of his *manumission*),[76] then 1 Clement would be sending a man in his seventies to Corinth! The situation is worse in the case of Valerius Vito. If we surmise with Lightfoot that he was a *libertus* of Claudius' third consort Valeria Messalina, he was freed no later than 48, the year Valeria died.[77] Always keeping in mind that Vito could have been older than thirty at his mistress's death, or even could have been freed before AD 48 if the Empress so decided, he would have probably been in his eighties in AD 96! It is somewhat difficult to believe that 1 Clement would have sent anyone nearly that old on the trying assignment to Corinth.

1.9 "Fortunatus" (1 Clement 65:1)

The last detail in this matter of the delegates is the fact that the third individual is called simply "Fortunatus." Since the Roman name ordinarily includes at least the

73 Ibid., 27. This precise point is repeated by William Jurgens in *The Faith of the Early Fathers*, p. 7, though Jurgens decides for a circa AD 80 dating, guessing that the "sudden calamities" of 1 Clement 1:1 may refer to the AD 79 eruption of Vesuvius. See also Lampe, *op. cit.*, pp. 153–155. Lampe calmly agrees that the names Claudius Ephebus and Valerius Vito do indeed signify that they are the manumitted slaves of the Emperor and his consort, while still dating 1 Clement "in den 90cr Jahren." Lampe makes no mention, though, of the lengthy time lapse between "the nineties" and their supposed manumission some forty to fifty years earlier.

74 Michael Grant, *The Roman Emperors*, 34.

75 For a fuller explanation of the custom regarding slaves' names, see Joel Schmidt, *Vie et Mort des esclaves dans la Rome antique*, 155f.

76 W. W. Buckland, *The Roman Law of Slavery*, 542.

77 M. Grant, *The Roman Emperors*, 34.

nomen and the *praenomen*, as in the case of the other two delegates, the fact that the third has a single name is strange. It is even more strange because Fortunatus was an extremely common name in the Imperial period, the practical equivalent of "John" today.[78] 1 Clement is not imprecise regarding a figure who, since he is an important representative on a sensitive mission, ought to have been precisely identified, if in fact this Fortunatus was a person already well known to the Corinthian community. To claim that this Fortunatus is the same mentioned by Paul in 1 Corinthians 16:17 may appear far-fetched.[79] Still, it would explain why 1 Clement would not have further identified this delegate. If it is the same Fortunatus as the one mentioned in 1 Corinthians, of course, the case for a circa AD 70 date is made all the stronger since that same Fortunatus would be going back to Corinth on a Church mission, a logical task for a person already known and presumably trusted at Corinth. On the other hand, if 1 Clement were written in circa AD 96, our Fortunatus would be some fifty years older than when he came to visit Paul, a most improbable eventuality. The late dating, though, would still have 1 Clement sending "John" on an important assignment, an odd omission to say the least.

1.10 Conclusion

Having taken into consideration the preceding eleven elements internal to the text of 1 Clement, the common dating hypothesis is seriously undermined for the following reasons:

1. There is very little evidence that the reference to "misfortunes" and "calamities" in 1 Clement 1 refers in any way to a persecution during the reign of the Emperor Domitian. In fact, there is very little evidence that there *was* a persecution during his reign!
2. The treatment of the Temple of Jerusalem in 1 Clement shows that the author uses it as an example within the context of a carefully arranged argument. It is referred to as an indication of the divine will for order. This *customary* order of which the Temple cult is such an epitome makes any use of the Greek historical present practically impossible. Thus the

78 The CIL has over one thousand entries for the masculine form of *Fortunatus* in Roman inscriptions alone! See CIL, VI, pars. 7, fasc. 11, pp. 2575–2580.

79 From 1 Corinthians 16:15 it is clear that Fortunatus is coming from Corinth to Rome, whereas 1 Clement 65:1 presumes he is traveling from Rome to Corinth. This is not necessarily a difficulty if we recall the extraordinarily frequent travel common between the two cities during the Imperial period (cf. Murphy-O'Connor, *St.Paul's Corinth*, esp. p. 98). Nor is Fortunatus' Latinate name any indication he was from Italy since Latin, and not Greek names predominate in pre-Hadrianic Corinthian inscriptions: p. 5; see also John Kent, Corinth VIII/3. *The Inscriptions* 1926–1950, p. 19. That Fortunatus *was* the same mentioned in 1 Corinthians 16 was argued by L. von Hertling, with further speculative application, in his "1 Kor 16,15 and 1 Clement 42", *Biblica* 20 (1939), pp. 276–283. This hypothesis was proposed by Edmundson, cf. *op. cit.*, p. 199: Robinson agrees in *op. cit.*, p. 333, and comments, "Of course it may not have been the same Fortunatus—though the fact that the only two we know of both came from Corinth looks like more than a coincidence."

present tenses used throughout the section require that the Temple, destroyed in AD 70, be standing at the time of the writing of 1 Clement. Further, any reference to a divinely willed order exemplified by the Temple is impossible after its destruction in the context of an argument against change in that order. Such a reference in circa AD 96 would have contradicted 1 Clement's whole argument that divinely willed order is unchangeable.

3. It is clear that some of the presbyters appointed by the Apostles are still alive as 1 Clement writes. If Paul is dead by AD 67, and 1 Clement writes in AD 96, a thirty year long period is necessary. The question is whether it is probable that the presbyters, already adults at their appointment, would have survived for thirty more years in the first century. This argument, with various differences, also applies to the issue of the emissaries.

Briefly, then, perhaps the position can best be stated this way: if, given the above specific questions relating to actual references in the text of 1 Clement, the currently accepted opinion were to hold that 1 Clement *was* written in circa AD 70, it is very doubtful that anyone would be able to dislodge it. The only argument for a late dating would be that this anonymous letter, which nowhere mentions monepiscopate, was composed by the Bishop of Rome, Clemens, because Eusebius says that he was bishop of Rome toward the end of the reign of Domitian. In such a case, everyone would admit that the circa AD 96 hypothesis would be precarious indeed.

Chapter Two
The New Testament and the Apostolic Fathers

If the thesis is to be defended that 1 Clement was written, not in circa AD 96 as almost everyone supposes, but in circa AD 70, it shall have to be tested not only on the basis of internal evidence, but also as regards the apparent relationship between 1 Clement and other first century Christian literature. We need to be able to show that there is nothing in the New Testament or in the other so-called Apostolic Fathers which would contradict the early-dating hypothesis. As will be seen from what follows, it will be argued that in some respects, 1 Clement shows little influence from the New Testament and the other early Christian literature. In some other ways, 1 Clement seems to be reflective of only early strains of Christian theological thought. In either case, it can be maintained that the very substance and form of expression found in 1 Clement puts backward pressure on any dating hypothesis since it can be shown in many ways to be quite primitive.

2.1 The New Testament

Regarding the New Testament, the logical first question comes to mind: what, if any, relationship does 1 Clement show to the New Testament? For many, this question has already been raised and admirably answered in the well received work of Donald A. Hagner, *The Use of the Old and New Testaments in Clement of Rome*. Hagner holds for quite a close relationship between the New Testament and 1 Clement and states, "Clement provides us with indications that the greater part if not the whole of the Pauline corpus was probably known to him and was present in his mind as he wrote in circa AD 95."[80] And again, "it may be said that we have evidence (slight though it be) that Clement probably knew one of the synoptics."[81]; and further, "the probability is heightened inasmuch as we know of no particular reason to believe that written copies of the Synoptic gospels were not already in possession (sic) of the leaders of the Church in the Empire's leading city."[82]

It is essential that this hypothesis be directly rebutted if the position is ever to be secured that 1 Clement wrote in circa AD 70. It seems unlikely that by 70, a Christian author in Rome would have at his disposal an entire collection of the Pauline corpus, not to mention copies of the Synoptic Gospels, which most scholars would agree were not yet all written.

80 Hagner, *op. cit.*, 237.

81 Ibid., 178.

82 Ibid.

It is important to note that Hagner alludes in his statements to the relationships of 1 Clement both to Paul and to the Synoptics, and that for him there is nothing surprising about 1 Clement having access to all these works by circa AD 95. This thought, it might be suggested, is father to the "discovery" of textual similarities between 1 Clement and various New Testament works. Upon analysis it can be shown that the evidence which Hagner actually presents, aside from the "probability" that 1 Clement would have been familiar with practically all the works of the New Testament, is slim indeed.

It is strange that Hagner could have come to such a conclusion about the Pauline corpus after having maintained the following: "There is no trace in Clement of a knowledge of 1 and 2 Thessalonians or of the Epistle to Philemon."[83] "Only for the first two books (Romans and 1 Corinthians) have we certain knowledge; for the others we must be content with various degrees of probability, (or) with mere possibility."[84] His affirmation, then, that there is "evidence" that the "greater part if not the whole" of the Pauline corpus was known to 1 Clement is almost wholly without foundation and probably prompted by his belief that 1 Clement was written in circa 95 when such an eventuality was at least a possibility.

The same can be said concerning his position on the relation between 1 Clement and the Synoptics. When read closely, Hagner actually admits, "in only one instance (i.e. the citation of Isaiah 29:13 in Mark 7:6 and in 1 Clement 15:2) does it seem at all probable that 1 Clement betrays a knowledge of the Synoptic Gospels."[85] Thus, any purported relationship between 1 Clement and the Synoptics is very weak, and made even weaker when it is recalled that, since Hagner's "evidence" has to do with a quote of *Isaiah* and not *per se* of *Mark*, all that proves is that 1 Clement may have been familiar with a particular version of Isaiah which was also known to Mark. It is likewise possible that what Hagner is calling "evidence" of 1 Clement's dependence on Mark, could be explained in other ways, including Mark's dependence on 1 Clement! Naturally, with the bias that 1 Clement was written in the mid-nineties, it did not occur to him that 1 Clement may have even ante-dated some of the Synoptics as well as other works of the New Testament, such as 1 Peter and Hebrews, with which it shows some similarity.[86]

---

83 Ibid., 237.

84 Ibid.

85 Ibid., 178.

86 Even if Hagner cannot be followed in his major thrust of finding close dependence of 1 Clement upon the Synoptics and the whole Pauline corpus, he does argue more cogently to great similarity between 1 Clement and other New Testament works, notably Hebrews (pp. 179–195); 1 Peter (pp. 239–248); James (pp. 248–256); and the Pastorals (pp. 230–237). His discussion is naturally too detailed to be summed up briefly and in a manner to show the actual parallels which Hagner finds. Suffice it to say that these kinds of similarities are precisely what one would expect to find in a first century Christian work. The similarities can be explained by saying he reflects a theological milieu which endures through the time of the other writings. Lightfoot, *op. cit.*, p. 353, also acknowledged the similarities between 1 Clement and Hebrews, 1 Peter, and James;

Ironically, however, Hagner's supposition is correct that *if* 1 Clement had been written in the nineties, there is a great possibility that he would have known the collected works of Paul and perhaps all of the Synoptics. Since it is virtually certain that he did *not* know these works and never quotes them even when it would have been extremely advantageous to his argument to have done so, all of this suggests that the early dating hypothesis is strengthened, and from a quarter where we would least have expected it.

If, then, there are no grounds for presuming *a priori* any necessary relationship, much less dependence, between 1 Clement and the New Testament, perhaps the best way to proceed will be to examine certain topical areas of New Testament interest in order to see what, if any, connection there may be with the thought of 1 Clement. The following issues will be singled out since it is obvious that no exhaustive analysis of the entire New Testament could be attempted in this limited space:

> The anti-Temple polemic in the New Testament; the Suffering Servant theme; the notion of church order in general; *πρεσβύ τερος, ἐπίσκοπος* and *ἀπόστολος;* eschatology, and finally, Apostolic Succession.

2.1.A *The Anti-Temple Polemic*

We have already seen that the issue of the Temple is a key one for dating 1 Clement. If one were satisfied that 1 Clement is using historical present tenses in chapters 40 and 41, one could simply see 1 Clement as referring to the Temple and its cult in so spiritualized a manner that its actual physical destruction would appear irrelevant. But when 1 Clement's approving sentiments about the Temple are compared to the New Testament, a further important objection arises. On the premise that 1 Clement wrote in the 90's even if one can hypothesize that he was not, for whatever reason, so dependent on the texts of the canonical Gospels and never quotes them, it is much more difficult to explain away 1 Clement's very positive attitude toward the Temple. It is insufficient to say that the Temple example helped his argument (which it does!), because that fails to shed any light on the dating question. One has to face the fact that certainly by the nineties the *theology* of the canonical Gospels was already widely known, even if the actual texts may have been still rare and not easily available. Regarding the Temple, then, it seems plausible to argue that after the Gospels were written, their clear anti-Temple attitude would have become

---

cf. also the opinion of Jerome below, no. 159. Following M. E. Boismard, "Clement de Rome et l'evangile de Jean", pp. 376–387; A. Jaubert, *op. cit.*, pp. 53ff., traced a number of parallel texts in John and 1 Clement. The similarities may be accounted for in several ways: liturgy, access to a common milieu, or some sort of literary dependence. She notes: "Entre l'évangile de Jean et la première épitre de Clément il n'existe, de l'aveu de tous, aucun rapprochement littéraire direct" (p. 53).

so widely known that even if an individual leader, like 1 Clement, disagreed with their *anti*-Temple sentiments, a *pro*-Temple loyalty would have been impossible to presume in a prospective audience, as 1 Clement does in chapters 40 and 41.

It is essential to recall that the anti-Temple attitude, which antedated its actual fall in AD 70, would have taken on the solidity of prophecy-come-true *after* AD 70. The Gospels then, whenever they were individually written, i.e. before or after AD 70, record a distinct judgment against the Temple and much of what it had come to stand for. Ignoring the plain fact that the Temple had in fact been destroyed would have been theologically unthinkable in AD 95–96.

Some examples are in order here, though, of course, the question of New Testament attitudes toward the Temple merits specific study of the kind not possible here.

In the trial scene before the high priest in Matthew 26:61, two false witnesses come forward and testify against Jesus saying, "This fellow said, 'I am able to destroy the Temple of God and to build it in three days.'" Mark's version follows a lengthy anti-Temple tirade including the cleansing in 11:15–19, ("Is it not written that my house shall be called a house of prayer for all nations? But you have made it a den of thieves."), the story of the widow's mites in 12:41–44,[87] then 13:2, "Do you see these great buildings? Not one stone shall be left upon another," and 13:14, "but when you see the abomination of desolation standing where it ought not, let the reader understand, then let those who are in Judea flee to the mountains." In 14:58 we have, "We heard him say, 'I will destroy this Temple that is made with hands and in three days I will build another not made with hands'." In Acts 6:13–14, Stephen's accusers testify. "This man does not cease to speak blasphemous words against this holy place and the law: for we have heard him say that this Jesus of Nazareth will destroy this place and change the customs which Moses delivered to us." In 7:48, the ultimate, "The Most High does not dwell in houses made by hands" (see John 2:13–22).

There is, then, in the canonical Gospels and Acts a fierce polemic against the Temple in which Jesus is portrayed as comparing it to a den of thieves and Stephen dies for the outrageous statement that God does not dwell there. Given the commonly accepted view that the writings of the Gospels and Acts followed a period of oral tradition and circulation of written sayings etc. which only later became written down in what we call the Gospels, two possibilities exist for the situation in AD 70: either the Gospels were written but yet not much circulated and not yet considered authoritative, or they were not yet written. The situation is quite distinct by AD 95–96: by then the anti-Temple polemic had proven shockingly prophetic when the Temple had indeed been destroyed. Again, for Clement to be writing in 95/96 and not know of this polemic, or to know of it and ignore it,

87 A. Wright, "The Widow's Mites—Praise or Lament? A Matter of Contexts," *CBQ* 44 (1981), 256–265.

is practically impossible precisely because by then the Temple was in ruins.[88] This further argument against the circa 96 dating of 1 Clement is necessarily somewhat recent since it depends on a more modern interpretation of the Gospels, their dating, and the process of their composition. Scarcely anyone today, though, would deny that the Gospel writer was also an accomplished theologian and that the anti-Temple attitude was a pervasive dimension of his theology.

On the other hand, if 1 Clement was written in circa AD 70 and knew of the anti-Temple polemical attitude of, say, Mark's Gospel, or even in the form it took in oral tradition of the time, he was free to ignore it. Certainly other Christians did so, notably those in the community at Jerusalem. Such neglect, though, whether in Rome or Jerusalem, made sense only so long as the Temple was standing. In AD 70 that Temple was burned to the ground. A pro-Temple attitude, at least as far as Christians were concerned, in the period after the Temple's destruction, not only would be in marked contrast with the growing conviction that the fate of Jerusalem and its Temple were God's judgement against the Old Testament in favor of the New Testament, such an attitude would also have the distinct air of unrealism since, in fact, there no longer *was* any Temple, nor cult nor sacrifice. In the context of 1 Clement's strategy to win over the Corinthians to a renewed sense of order in their community, any reference to a Temple which stood in ruins would simply make no sense, as has already been shown. It is easier to believe that 1 Clement wrote while the Temple still stood, i.e. in circa AD 70.

2.1.B The Suffering Servant

The point made in the previous section was that 1 Clement seems wholly unaware of a strain in early Christian theology which found broad expression in the written Gospels. His lack of knowledge of the anti-Temple polemic was interpreted to suggest that perhaps 1 Clement was composed while the Temple was still intact and the anti-Temple polemical attitude had not yet been fuelled by the events of AD 70.

88 It is interesting to note that Paul, for all his anti-Law argumentation, could nevertheless also draw practical parallels from the Temple practice which still thrived when he wrote. See 1 Corinthians 10:15. Even though Jaubert, *op. cit.*, p. 20, was convinced that 1 Clement was written between AD 95 and 98, nevertheless she also recognized the inherent difficulty which arises from the fact that 1 Clement is so positive vis-a-vis Judaism. She comments, *en passant*: "Le principal argument qu'on ait invoqué contre l'origine juive de Clément, c'est l'absence dans l'épître de toute allusion aux problèmes juifs du temps. Aucune discussion sur le légalisme juif (sabbat, circoncision); il ne semble pas que l'auteur ait ressenti dans la chair le conflit des observances; le peuple juif actuel est comme inexistant. Or, par ailleurs, Clément assume hardiment l'héritage d'Israël et toujours de manière positive. Il y a là un paradoxe qui n'est pas complètement éclairci, car il paraît invraisemblable qu'à la fin du premier siècle de notre ere la communauté juive de Rome et la communauté chrétienne n'aient pas eu de rapports difficiles" (p. 30). The "paradox" disappears, however, if one reads the epistle as having been written prior to the escalation of the Jewish-Christian hostilities in the wake of the fall of Jerusalem, i.e. AD 70.

The point of this section is practically the reverse: we find in 1 Clement evidence of a strikingly *similar* theology of the Suffering Servant which he *shares* with the written Gospels, although he never quotes any of them. The Suffering Servant theme forms part of the complex background of the development of what later become the Gospels' Passion narratives.[89] First Clement's direct citation of the Suffering Servant poem of Isaiah 53:1–12 forms the largest part of 1 Clement 16:

> 3. Lord, who has believed our report, and to whom was the arm of the Lord revealed? We declared him before the Lord as a child, as a root in thirsty ground; there is no form in him, nor glory, and we saw him, and he had neither form nor beauty, but his form was without honor, less than the form of a man, a man living among stripes and toil, and acquainted with the endurance of weakness, for his face was turned away, he was dishonoured, and not esteemed. 4. He it is who beareth our sins, and is pained for us, and we regarded him as subject to pain, and stripes and affliction, 5. but he was wounded for our sins and he has suffered for our iniquities. The chastisement of our peace was upon him; with his bruises we were healed. 6. All we like sheep went astray in his path, 7. and the Lord delivered him up for our sins, and he opened not his mouth because of his affliction. As a sheep he was brought to the slaughter, and as a dumb lamb before its shearer, so he opened not his mouth. In humiliation his judgment was taken away. 8. Who shall declare his generation? For his life is taken away from the earth. 9. For the iniquities of my people is he come to death. 10. And I will give the wicked for his burial and the rich for his death; for he wrought no iniquity, nor was guile found in his mouth. And the Lord's will is to purify him from stripes. 11. If ye make an offering for sin, your soul shall see a long-lived seed. 12. And the Lord's will is to take of the toil of his soul, to show him light and to form him with understanding, to justify a righteous man who serveth many well. And he himself shall bear their sins. 13. For this reason shall he inherit many, and he shall share the spoils of the strong; because his soul was delivered to death, and he was reckoned among the transgressors. 14. And he bore the sins of many, and for their sins was he delivered up.

89 P. Grelot considers the question *ex professo* in *Les Poêmes du Serviteur*, pp. 138ff. Obviously, the text of Isaiah 53 is at the basis of Paul's treatment in 1 Corinthians 15:3–4, which makes its appearance in 1 Clement no surprise since 1 Clement 47 shows his explicit dependence on 1 Corinthians.

This lengthy quote is followed by an equally poignant Old Testament reference which early Christians probably used as an object of their meditations on the suffering and death of Jesus. These meditations in turn influenced the composition of the Passion narratives. First Clement quotes Psalm 22:

> 15. But I am a worm and no man, a reproach of men, and despised of the people. 16. All they who saw me mocked me, they spoke with their lips, they shook their heads: He hoped on the Lord, let him deliver him, let him save him for he hath pleasure in him.

First Clement's rhetorical purpose for the use of these texts is made clear from v. 17: "You see, Beloved, what is the example which is given to us; for if the Lord was humble-minded, etc."[90] However, the purpose for mentioning these texts here is to note that there is considerable evidence that the Passion narratives were themselves based on precisely such theological reflection as 1 Clement presents.[91] We have long accepted the thesis that the Gospel writers present their interpretation of Jesus as the Christ in light of a profound reflection on the meaning of the Old Testament.[92] Luke's famous episode in 24:13ff. of the two disciples on the road to Emmaus gives evidence that the early Christian faith in the identity of Jesus as

---

90 Again, 1 Clement seems very close to Paul's Philippians 2:4ff.: "Have this mind among yourselves which was in Christ Jesus, who, though he was in the form of God, he humbled himself and became obedient unto death ..." On the point of 1 Clement's christology, especially as regards its relationship to Paul, Jaubert, *op. cit.*, p. 71, observes: "On n'en déduira naturellement pas que Clément était insensible aux développements pauliniens, mais on pourra penser qu'il ne les avait guère assimilés." On the point of whether 1 Clement shows much theological development, she adds: "La religion de Clément est celle de l'Ancien Testament" (p. 73). Finally, she notes: "Il ne faut pas demander à Clément de synthèse théologique. On le jugera souvent plus archaïque que Paul et Jean" (p. 75). I should again add that Jaubert was convinced 1 Clement was nevertheless written in ca. AD 95–98 (p. 20).

91 Grelot emphasizes the intimate connection between the thought of Isaiah 52:13–53:12 and Psalm 2: "L'intéret se concentre spécialement autour d'Is 52,12–53,12, où la Passion de Jésus est le filigranne du texte, exactement comme elle est lue dans le texte du Psaume 22 d'après Matthew 27,39–50."

92 R. Fuller in his *The Foundations of New Testament Christology* treats the question *passim*. On p. 153, he says, "The very earliest Son of Man Christology was intended to assert that the soteriological significance of Jesus' ministry radically called into question by Jesus' crucifixion ... was triumphantly vindicated by the resurrection." The point, of course, is that somewhere between the crucifixion and the actual writing of the Gospels, this development of Christology had to have taken place. Fuller, p. 153, continues, "Perhaps the earliest line of thought was not derived from Isaiah 53, but from the atoning significance of the death of the martyrs. ... Once, however, this step had been taken, it was not long before Isaiah 53 was brought in, as we see from Mark 10:45b and Mark 14:24." It hardly needs to be demonstrated that the connection between the Old Testament and the composition of the Gospels has been commonplace in recent scholarship. For a classical approach, see R. Bultmann, *History of the Synoptic Tradition*, pp. 462 *et passim*; for particular application to the Passion Narratives, cf. ibid., pp. 275ff.; cf. also V. Taylor, "The Origin of the Markan Passion Sayings," in *New Testament Essays*, pp. 70–71.

Messiah is based on an interpretation of the Old Testament as prophesying about Jesus. This was particularly important in coming to understand the apparent paradox that Jesus was a suffering Messiah. In this section of 1 Clement, although he still does not give any sign of knowing the actual written Gospels, he does show familiarity with certain key Old Testament texts which were instrumental in enabling the Gospel writers to compose their Gospels. First Clement, then, may be an early reflection of what has long been hypothesized as an essential prerequisite for eventual composition of the written Gospels, namely the theological identification of such Old Testament texts as Isaiah 53 and Psalm 22 as sources for coming to the faith that Jesus, not only despite but even through his suffering, revealed himself as the Anointed One of God. If so, this theology which antedated the writing of the Gospels would not be at all out of place in a Christian work written prior to them, or at least prior to the time they were widely circulated.[93] If on the other hand 1 Clement was written in circa AD 95 when all the Gospels had been composed and when surely some of them had circulated in Roman circles for some time, why would he not have alluded to the written Gospel testimony to Jesus' suffering and example of humility?

Following closely upon the issue of the use of the Suffering Servant is 1 Clement's more general use of the term *παῖς* to refer to Jesus. He does this three times in succession in chapter 59:

> 2: But we shall be innocent of this sin, and will pray with eager entreaty and supplication that the Creator of the Universe may guard unhurt the number of his elect that has been numbered in all the world through his beloved child (*παιδὸς αὐτοῦ*) Jesus Christ, through whom he called us from darkness to light, from ignorance to the full knowledge of the glory of his name.
>
> 3: Thou dost multiply nations upon earth and hast chosen out from them all those that love thee through Jesus Christ thy beloved child. (*παιδός*)
>
> 4: Let all nations know thee, that thou art God alone, and that Jesus Christ is thy child (ὁ παῖς σου)

In these three instances we have clear evidence of a very early stage in Christian christology which referred to Jesus as the *παις Του θεου. Παῖς* in Greek can be translated as servant or child and thus was the LXX choice to translate the

93 Conveniently enough for the point of view of this thesis, on p. 98, W. G. Kummel in his *Introduction to the New Testament* (1975), reviews the current dating hypotheses for the dating of Mark and concludes, "Since no overwhelming argument for the years before or after 70 can be adduced, we must content ourselves with saying that Mark was written ca. 70."

ebed Yahweh of the Servant poems of the Old Testament. Regarding its antiquity, Cullmann has this to say:

> The Book of Acts proves that in the earliest times of Primitive Christianity there existed an explanation of the person and work of Jesus which we may designate somewhat incorrectly as Christology of the "Servant of God", more correctly we could call it "Paidology." We could even go further and assert that this is probably the earliest solution of the Christological question. ... There are four passages of this kind (in Acts); it is significant that all four occur in the same section, in chapters 3 and 4, and that Jesus is called παῖς τοῦ θεοῦ in no other book of the New Testament. The expression here is Jesus-Pais, exactly as one will be accustomed later to say Jesus-Christ. It is becoming a proper name, just as occurred in the case of the word Christ. This confirms the existence of a very early Christology on the basis of which Jesus was called *ebed Yahweh*. It will disappear in the following period, but its use must reach back into the very earliest times.[94]

Cullmann is implying here that this usage of παῖς to refer to Jesus is so ancient that it is preserved only in four scant passages in Acts. By the time the New Testament itself is composed, the term has already been supplanted by Χριστός as the preferred title for Jesus. Thus, παῖς is a very ancient designation indeed. How then are we to explain 1 Clement's three usages?

On one hand, we know that 1 Clement postdates Paul. Already in Paul the term Χριστός has supplanted the usage of παῖς. So, it cannot be that 1 Clement was written in the most ancient period of Christological development.[95] The probable answer lies in the fact that the three usages of παῖς occur in a prayer. The liturgical formula preserved the most ancient designation. Still, we can admit with Jaubert that 1 Clement's christology is primitive indeed, and not yet so developed as in other sections of the New Testament. This, in turn, is just what we would expect in a work written early, before the New Testament was composed. The date could very well be circa AD 70 once again.

94 Cullmann, *Peter*, 66.

95 J. N. D. Kelly in his *Early Christian Creeds*, p. 140, when treating of the title "Christos" notes that in the post-apostolic age the title had to be explained to converts entering the Church from a Gentile environment. In contrast, Clement uses the word *Christos* more frequently with the article than without and "it is apparent that it retained for him something of its Messianic flavour."

2.1.C *Jesus Christ as High Priest*

It is well known that in the entire New Testament only in Hebrews is Jesus called ἀρχιερεύς. First Clement calls him ἀρχιερεύς in 36:1: τὸν ἀρχιερέα τῶν προσφορῶν ἡμῶν. It might be thought that here we have a contradiction to the previous point that 1 Clement's christology is primitive.

To begin with, it will be admitted that primitiveness, like "earliness" or "lateness", is in itself quite a relative term. The implied question is: primitive as compared with what?

In the last section it was shown that 1 Clement, like Acts 3 and 4, maintains a use of παῖς to describe Jesus. This was in contrast to the Gospels which never describe him as such. On the other hand, Hebrews exhibits a rich and exalted christology which is surely a development over the understanding that Jesus's followers had of him during the public ministry or immediately after the resurrection in circa AD 29.

Central to the issue here, then, is how "late" is Heb? For our purposes here it will perhaps be sufficient to note that, while difficult to date with precision, a serious argument can be made to date Hebrews in circa AD 68.[96] Thus, while a christology in which Jesus is conceived of as high priest may well be "later" than the "paidology" described above, it is not so late as to prevent our dating 1 Clement to circa AD 70.

2.1.D *Church Order*

It has been urged by many that the original order in the Christian community, to the extent that it can be called order at all, was charismatic rather than structured in any specific, normative or official way. In fact, it is the Corinthian community above all which is viewed as a kind of paradigm of this charismatic community experience.[97]

---

96 A. Vanhoye's summary of the dating of Hebrews deserves to be quoted in full: "La tradition ancienne a rangé l'épître aux Hébreux parmi les épîtres pauliniennes, tout en reconnaissant que son texte grec n'était pas de l'apôtre Paul. La critique moderne n'a pas les moyens de déterminer avec certitude les circonstances de sa composition et hésite pour sa datation entre la fin du règne de Claude (mort en 54), les dernières années de Néron (mort en 69) et le règne de Domitien (8196). La première position a peu de partisans. L'ensemble des données favorise plutôt, à mon avis, la deuxième position: l'épître paraît avoir été composée par un compagnon de Paul quelque temps avant que n'éclate la guerre juive des années 66–70, qui entraîna la destruction du Temple de Jérusalem." *Prêtres anciens, Prêtre nouveau selon le Nouveau Testament*, p. 82, no. 5.

97 M. Bourke, "Reflections on Church Order in the New Testament," 508: "I think it can be fairly said that Kung's enthusiasm for the Church of Corinth, one which he shares with Kasemann and Schweizer, is the reason for a certain weakness in his presentation of the church order. While he admits the development of order, and the association of the charism with ordination, there can be little doubt that Kung idealizes Corinth." Cf. H. F. von Campenhausen, Kirchliches Amt and geistliche Vollmacht in den ersten drei Jahrhunderten, (1953), 69: "The Church with Paul is therefore not regarded as an organization constituted in some way with ranks and grades, but as a single living cosmos of free spiritual gifts which serve and complete one another, but whose

This question shall be taken up again later, but for the moment we may rightly ask how the conception of church order in 1 Clement compares with that of the New Testament. If the New Testament shows *no* sign of church order, then the structural interests of 1 Clement would logically have to be seen as a much later development.

One objective way to approach this question would be to concentrate on the Pauline epistles, since they were composed before AD 70. To discover whether Paul was interested in church order, it may be helpful to discover how often he refers to the problem of *disorder* in the local churches and to the consequent need to resolve disorder in favor of order and unity.

In Romans 14 Paul addresses the vexed question of whether it is licit to eat meat which has been offered to idols. The issue, though it may appear quaint and unimportant to modern eyes, was a critical one for a community composed of converts from paganism and Judaism, and in fact threatened to tear the Roman church apart.

> 14:3: Let not him who eats despise him who abstains, and let not him who abstains pass judgement on him who eats.
> 10: Why do you pass judgement on your brother? Or you, why do you despise your brother?
> 13: Then let us no more pass judgment on one another, but rather decide never to put a stumbling block or hindrance in the way of a brother.
> 15: If your brother is being injured by what you eat, you are no longer walking in love.

Thus it is evident that Paul thought he had to intervene in this community dispute. He justified the intervention with these words:

> 15:15–16: But on some points I have written to you very boldly by way of reminder, because of the grace given me by God to be a minister of Christ Jesus to the Gentiles in the priestly service of the gospel of God, so that the offering

---

bearers can never rise above one another or shut themselves off against one another. To the extent that all compulsion and all lasting authority to command is expressly excluded, the picture of Church that emerges, understood in the sense of a human social order, is utopian." In a similar vein, J. G. Gager, *Kingdom and Community*, p. 69: "One unusual aspect of early Christianity is that its antinomian energies persisted as long as they did. Or, to put the matter more cautiously, the process of consolidation did not set in with full vigor until the second half of the first century, and even then it was resisted actively by a number of individuals and communities. In this sense one might say that there were two outbursts of charismatic authority—Jesus himself and some of the early converts on Gentile soil."

> of the Gentiles may be acceptable, sanctified by the Holy Spirit.

It is clear that Paul sees this ministry as having been given him by God. Such examples of dissension in the community, which Paul vividly describes and forcefully opposes in the communities of his own day to which he wrote can be easily multiplied.

> Romans 16:17–18: I appeal to you, brethren, to take note of those who create dissensions and difficulties, in opposition to the doctrine which you have been taught: avoid them. For such persons do not serve our Lord Christ, but their own appetites, and by fair and flattering words they deceive the hearts of the simpleminded.
>
> 1 Corinthians 1:10ff: I appeal to you brethren by the name of our Lord Jesus Christ, that all of you agree and that there be no dissensions among you, but that you be united in the same mind and the same judgment.
>
> 2 Corinthians 13:1ff: Any charge must be sustained by the evidence of two or three witnesses. I warned those who sinned before and all the others, and I warn them now while absent, as I did when present on my second visit, that if I come again I will not spare them. 9. What we pray for is your improvement. I write this while I am away from you, in order that when I come I may not have to be severe in my use of the authority which the Lord has given me for building up and not for tearing down.

Thus Paul, whose authentic letters are the earliest evidence we have of the conditions which prevailed in primitive Christianity, was vitally interested in preserving order or in restoring it wherever it had been disturbed.

The method he chose to accomplish this is none other than by an appeal to the unity of the gospel message itself and by a personal ministry of governance. He was himself an example of the fact that personal authority was indeed exercised in the early Church. His very letter-writing was itself a "structure" by means of which the errors or centrifugal forces within the community were corrected or neutralized.

Perhaps in no case is this more clear than in 1 Corinthians, the very letter which 1 Clement mentions by name and of which he was, therefore, certainly fully cognizant. Like Romans, 1 Corinthians begins by identifying Paul as "called by the will of God to be an apostle of Christ Jesus." Almost immediately, Paul launches into an appeal for unity and freedom from dissension. This is precisely the passage which has come to the mind of 1 Clement and no wonder: the dissension is caused by conflicting allegiances, one group saying they belong to Paul, another to Cephas, or to Apollos. This allegiance, so destructive of ecclesial unity as it was, originated in the fact that particular Apostles had baptized various groups in the Corinthian Church. (Since the factionalism came immediately on the heels of the baptism of new converts, when was the intervening time of structureless charisms?) The divisions were unwittingly caused by the spontaneous allegiances generated by a natural attachment to the preachers who first told them of the faith and then baptized them. Perhaps there were differences in nuance between Paul, Cephas, and Apollos' modes of preaching the faith, but it is difficult now to trace these. Whatever the case, Paul shows no interest, or even knowledge, of what these differences may have been, but is extremely concerned that the unity of the Church be restored. While the Apostles themselves traveled on, leaving their baptized converts behind, there can be no question that in the converts' minds the leader-follower structure was already implicit in the process whereby they had become converts in the first place.

It may be objected that this is still the charismatic period and that there is no evidence in Paul of the ἐπίσκοπος—πρεσβύτερος structure. Perhaps not explicitly, but there is further evidence of structure in the Corinthian convert community.

In 1 Corinthians 3:5 Paul asks, "What then is Apollos, what is Paul? Servants through whom you believed, as the Lord assigned to each." The passive sense of the concept "assignment" is unmistakable. Again, in v. 10, "According to the commission of God given to me, like a skilled builder I laid a foundation and another man is building upon it." In vv. 22ff, "whether Paul or Apollos or Cephas ... all are yours. And you are Christ's and Christ is God's." This summary description of the fundamental relationship between the members of the Corinthian Church, those who preached to them, Christ and God forms a chain-like design quite similar to the famous "Apostolic Succession" passage of 1 Clement 42:1ff.:

> The Apostles received the Gospel for us from the Lord Jesus Christ. Jesus Christ was sent from God. The Christ is from God and the Apostles from the Christ.

Certainly the situations which Paul and 1 Clement faced were distinct, but there is so close a resemblance between the ways in which they develop an answer to the diverse questions which they were tackling, that the impression is hard to resist that Paul and 1 Clement had identical views at least as regards the basis of the fundamental structure of the Church: it comes from God himself, through Christ and from him, through the Apostles to the faithful. While the concrete specifications of this fundamental structure could and would change, the furthest thing from the minds of both these men was that the unity and order of the Church was somehow optional, haphazard, or spontaneous.

Regarding preaching the gospel, in 1 Corinthians 9:16-17 Paul says:

> For if I preach the gospel that gives me no ground for boasting. For necessity is laid upon me. For if I do this of my own will, I have a reward; but if not of my own will, I am entrusted with a commission.

Again, there is no question that the very preaching of the gospel is a task assigned to Paul by the Lord. At the end of the discourse on the Eucharist in 1 Corinthians 11:34 he notes, "About the other things I will give directions when I come."

Chapter 12 of 1 Corinthians introduces the topic of the "spiritual gifts" (*πνευματικῶν*).

In v. 4, the RSV has "There are varieties of gifts, but one spirit." "Gifts" is *χαρισμάτων*. The key is in v. 7 where it explicitly says, "To each is given (*δίδοται*) , the manifestation of the Spirit for the common good." In v. 11, after a list of the various "gifts", Paul says, "All these are inspired by one and the same Spirit, who apportions to each one individually as he wills."

In the following fable about the parts of the body, Paul says, in 1 Corinthians 12:18, "God arranged the organs of the body, each one of them, as he chose." In vv. 27ff:

> Now you are the body of Christ and individually members of it. And God has appointed in the Church, first apostles, second prophets, third teachers, then workers of miracles, then healers, administrators, speakers, in various kinds of tongues. Are all apostles? Are all prophets? ...

Thus, the early Corinthian community, according to Paul, knew of a certain structure in the community, a structure which is, in every case, founded on the gifts, or the commission or the appointment of God. This whole section implies that there *was* disagreement within the Corinthian church that things should be ordered this way. Paul continues giving rules and regulations about prophesying and speaking in tongues, concluding in 1 Corinthians 14:33, "God is not a God of confusion but of peace." He gives orders that women are to remain silent in the assembly. He does not say these things lightly: v. 37: "If any one thinks that he is a prophet, or spiritual, he should acknowledge that what I am writing is a command of the Lord." This, again, seems to echo what 1 Clement says in 63:2: "For you will give us joy and gladness if you are obedient to the things which we have written through the Holy Spirit."

In 1 Corinthians 16:1, Paul says, "Now concerning the contribution for the saints: as I directed the churches of Galatia, so you also are to do." There can be no question that, at least in Paul's own mind, his role as Apostle and preacher of the gospel also includes giving concrete directions to the community. He likewise directs that the community be submissive (ὑποτάσσησθε) to Stephanas in 1 Corinthians 16:16 as well as to others.

While on one hand it is clear that 1 Corinthians was written to the very first generation of the Corinthian Church, it also is clear that there quickly appeared a number of causes of dissension. The dissension seems, at least in part, to have to do with the exact roles each of the new Christians was to play in the community. It is also equally clear that Paul, the Apostle, does not hesitate to establish directives, even to the point of bidding the Corinthians to be submissive to some of their own number.

The situation in 2 Corinthians is not much different. Again, the first verse introduces "Paul, an apostle of Christ Jesus, by the will of God." In 1:21 it is again God who "establishes us with you and who has commissioned us." In 2:17, "For we are not, like so many, peddlers of God's word, but as men of sincerity, as commissioned by God, in the sight of God we speak in Christ." In 3:4–6, "Such is the confidence we have through Christ toward God. Not that we are sufficient of ourselves to claim anything as coming from us; our sufficiency is from God who has qualified us to be ministers (διακόνους) of a new covenant." In 4:1, "Therefore, having this ministry (διακονίαν) by the mercy of God." In 5:18, "All this is from God who, through Jesus Christ, gave us the ministry (διακονίαν) of reconciliation." In 5:20, "We are ambassadors for Christ, God making his appeal through us." In 8:6–18 "Accordingly we have urged Titus that he should also complete our appeal, but being very earnest he is going to you of his own accord. With him we are sending the brother who is famous for his preaching of the gospel." In 8:22, "And with them we are sending our brother whom we have often tested and found earnest in many matters." In 8:23ff, "As for Titus, he is my partner and fellow worker in your service; as for our brethren, they are messengers (ἀπόστολοι) of the Churches, the glory of Christ." In 10:8, "For even if I boast a little too much of our authority (τῆς ἐξουσίας ἡμῶν) which the Lord gave for building you up and not for destroying you, I shall not be put to shame."

Several interesting things appear in these passages. First, Paul carefully distinguishes between his use of the first person singular (referring to himself) and the first person plural, indicating what he shares with Timothy, likewise a sender of the epistle (1:1). This is significant because already Paul shows that the authority he has been given by the Lord (13:10) he shares with Timothy (10:8). (It is to be noted that no serious commentator has doubted the authenticity of 2 Corinthians.) This shared power is likewise communicated to others (8:23) who have become Apostles, sent this time, not by the Lord but by Paul (8:17, 22). Paul's ministry is throughout a διακονία. Again, there is the constant dimension of the Lord sending, giving, commissioning. Conversely, Paul is sent, commissioned, given, etc.

In short, by the restricted use of these three, indubitably authentic letters, the ones most probably known to the author of 1 Clement,[98] it can be shown that structure *per se*, is not only not foreign to the Corinthian community prior to 1 Clement, it actually existed in the days when Paul himself ministered, personally or from afar, to the Corinthian Church. The assertion, then, that any and all structure or interest in it is indicative of a late letter simply does not do justice to the texts of the epistles themselves. Obviously this argument would have particular application to other New Testament works, especially the Pastorals, but that does not concern us directly here.

If then it can be granted that sure signs of structure can be seen in Romans, 1 and 2 Corinthians, the modern argument should be concerned with, not the *existence* of structure, but with the *degree of development* of structure and the question of whether or not a particular degree of development should be considered *normative*. From the perspective of 1 Clement, the issue is whether or not his overall interest in structure is in itself sufficient to decide that the letter is late. The above mentioned texts from Paul show the exact opposite: an interest in structure is manifested by the Apostle himself, and must therefore be admitted as a very early phenomenon in Christianity.

2.1.E Ἀπόστολος

When one speaks of church order in Paul, or for that matter throughout the New Testament, the touchstone for establishing the principal means whereby order and unity were established in the community must be the apostle. At all strata of the New Testament is the apostle in evidence: in Paul, in the Synoptics, in Acts, 1 and 2 Peter, Jude, the Pastorals, and in the Apocalypse.

For the purposes of our discussion, however, it is perhaps better to continue to concentrate on Paul since he is the earliest contributor to the New Testament. In some ways, Paul's conviction of his own apostleship is a proof *par excellence* that an interest in structure and church order is not incompatible with the earliest strata of New Testament thought.

While Paul's zeal for the gospel and the conviction he had of its importance are not to be doubted, it was his underlying confidence that he was an authentic apostle that made his preaching and letter writing able to have the effect they did on the formative period of the Church's life. In Galations 1:1, he writes:

---

98 Cf. Kummel, *op. cit.*, p. 287ff. In light of the above critique of Hagner, caution has to be exercised here. Of 1 Clement's knowledge of 1 Corinthians we are certain because he mentions it explicitly and proves by his references to Apollos and the situation in Corinth that he is indeed referring to the canonical 1 Corinthians. For Hagner's argument supporting 1 Clement's knowledge of Romans. Cf. Hagner, *op. cit.*, pp. 214ff. The problem regarding 2 Corinthians is more complicated. First Clement mentions Paul's letter, perhaps implying he was unaware that Paul had written more than one to the Corinthians. In any case, my point in all of this is that Paul certainly shows an interest in church structure, and this in the certainly authentic 1 and 2 Corinthians and Romans, all three of which 1 Clement may have known himself.

> Paul, an apostle not from men nor through man, but through Jesus Christ and God the Father.

In 1:12, he writes in a similar vein referring to his gospel:

> For I neither received it from man, nor was I taught it, but it came through the revelation of Jesus Christ.

In Romans 1:1:

> Paul, a servant of Jesus Christ, called to be an apostle ... concerning Jesus Christ, through whom we have received grace and apostleship.

In 1 Corinthians 9:1:

> Am I not free? Am I not an apostle? Have I not seen Jesus our Lord? Are not you my workmanship in the Lord? If to others I am not an apostle, at least I am to you; for you are the seal of my apostleship in the Lord.

In 2 Corinthians 11:5:

> I think I am not in the least inferior to these superlative apostles.

In Philippians 1:16:

> I am put here for the defense of the gospel.

As we know, the word ἀπόστολος comes from the Greek ἀποστέλλω and means "one who is sent." It is clear from Paul's formulations that he never forgot this passive dimension of his apostleship; he received it, he was called, was appointed, was put here, all because God willed it so. Paul summed it up well in Romans 10:14–15:

> How then shall they call on him in whom they have not believed? And how shall they believe in him whom they have not heard? And how shall they hear without a preacher? And how shall they preach unless they are sent?

Thus there can be no doubt whatever that Paul of Tarsus saw himself as an Apostle sent on a mission to preach the gospel. This characteristic presence in Paul of consciousness of being an Apostle is certain evidence of the fact of his leadership in the early Church, and therefore incontrovertible evidence of structure.

In the foregoing, the establishment of the fact that Paul acted as an *Apostle* was with a view to rebut the argument that the early Church was a wholly charismatic organization with no structural elements. Paul's apostleship more than anything else shows that that cannot be sustained.

As we turn to 1 Clement, however, the issue of apostleship changes slightly. We can take for granted that the Apostle was a well-established figure in the Church, whenever 1 Clement was written. But interesting is the fact that 1 Clement knows of only *two* Apostles by name, Peter and Paul. He shows this in chapter 5, which was examined above in detail. In no other passage of 1 Clement do we have mention of any other Apostles. In 44, which we shall examine below for another reason, 1 Clement reminisces about the fact that the presbyters were appointed by the Apostles, "or later on by other eminent men," showing that he does not indiscriminately call others Apostles. In 47, he refers explicitly to the episode from 1 Corinthians when Paul had to chide the Corinthians for siding either with him, or with Apollos or with Cephas. Then he says, v. 4:

> But that partisanship entailed less guilt on you; for you were partisans of Apostles of high reputation, and of a man approved by them.

Here he shows again a careful distinction between the Apostles Peter and Paul, and Apollos who was not an Apostle. As we saw above, the question is this: if 1 Clement had been written in circa AD 95, how is it that he would only recognize two Apostles, and not, for example, the Twelve which would by then have already been a Synoptic tradition? The question in some ways is unanswerable, but again, it may put backward pressure on any dating hypothesis for 1 Clement.

2.1.F Ἐπίσκοπος–πρεσβύτερος

One question which must be examined in particular is the use of the terms "ἐπίσκοπος" and "πρεσβύτερος." It is true that Paul never uses either word in the epistles generally accepted as being authentically Pauline, with the single exception of the opening address of the Philippians where the epistle is addressed to "ἐπισκό ποις καὶ διακόνοις." This exact combination is found in 1 Clement 42:4–5:

> They preached from district to district and from city to city, and they appointed their first converts, testing them by the Spirit, to be bishops and deacons (ἐπισκόπους καὶ διακόνους) of the future believers. And this was no new method, for many years before had bishops and deacons been written of: for the Scripture says in one place, "I will establish their bishops with righteousness and their deacons with faith."

It is essential here to determine, as far as we can, what exactly Paul and 1 Clement meant by "*ἐπίσκοποι.*"[99] It is anachronous and misleading to translate the word by the modern English, "bishops."[100] "Bishop", as it is used everywhere today, refers to an individual who is given principal governance of a local church, and who is superior in rank to the presbyterate. The fact is, both in Paul, elsewhere in the New Testament and in 1 Clement, the term *ἐπίσκοπος* is the conceptual equivalent of *presbyteros* and by no means suggests single or "monepiscopal" government as it would at a later date in Church history. The very fact that *ἐπίσκοπος* appears so often in the plural, suggests we are dealing here with a group or college of *ἐπίσκοποι* and not an individual. Acts 20:28 , in the middle of Paul's speech to the *πρεσβύτεροι* of Ephesus, he calls them *ἐπίσκοποι.* "Take heed to yourselves and to all the flock, in which the Holy Spirit has made you guardians (*ἐπισκόπους*)." This same usage is found in 1 Timothy 3:1: "If anyone aspires to the office of bishop (sic RSV) (*ἐπισκοπῆς*)," while it is clear that he is referring to the same people when he calls them elders in 5:17: "Let the elders (*πρεσβύτεροι*) who rule well."

If we were to ask whether anyone in Paul's time exercised what the Church would later call monepiscopacy, we might rightly look, not to these *ἐπίσκοποι*, but to Paul himself. While not long resident in any given local community, it was his personal directions which were definitive in all of the churches which he founded or to whom he would later write. In other words, if one is looking for an individual overseer, and that is what *ἐπίσκοπος* means etymologically, then Paul may be considered, if not in name, still in fact the *ἐπίσκοπος.*

To sum up this material briefly, we can conclude that Paul, prior to his death in the mid-60's, knew and approved of *ἐπίσκοποι καὶ διάκονοι* at Philippi; Acts, while it often uses the term *πρεσβύτεροι*, in this speech attributed to Paul, refers to them as *ἐπίσκοποι.* First Timothy, no matter whether it may be pseudonymous, still preserves the archaic title of *ἐπίσκοπος* when what is undoubtedly meant is *πρεσβύτεροι* and asserts that this is in the Pauline tradition. Thus, the fluid interchange of the terms *ἐπίσκοποι* and *πρεσβύτεροι* may preserve a very early stratum of ecclesial terminology.

---

99 Cf. B. F. Streeter, *The Primitive Church*, p. 215: "As in Philippians, bishops and deacons are the names of two kinds of officers. These two officers are spoken of by Clement in a way which excludes the possibility that presbyters is the name of a third intermediate office. ... There is nothing to call forth surprise in this evidence that in Rome and Corinth a system still prevailed not very far removed from that established by Paul."

100 For a striking contemporary example of serious misunderstanding of this elementary problem, see, *Baptism, Eucharist and Ministry*, (BEM), Faith and Order Paper No. 111, World Council of Churches, Geneva, 1982, p. 29: "Clement of Rome linked the mission of the bishop with the sending of Christ by the Father and the sending of the apostles by Christ. This made the bishop the successor of the apostles, ensuring the permanence of the apostolic mission in the Church." But 1 Clement nowhere mentions or even alludes to bishops!

The fact that this interchangeability is precisely what we find in 1 Clement, makes even more plausible the thesis that we are dealing here with an early and not a late first-century work.

Although Paul himself never uses the term πρεσβύτερος, we should likewise ask if he did not refer to the presbyterate implicitly when he refers in 1 Corinthians to Stephanas and the submission of the Corinthians which is owed to him and others like him.

If Paul wrote 1 Corinthians in the middle-fifties, as most scholars would hold, we are still talking about a fifteen year period before AD 70.[101] The community, with its ever-present need for guidance, would have grown during that time, as would certain community customs. If Stephanas is a designated leader already in the fifties, is it not possible that he and men like him were by 70 already referred to as πρεσβύτεροι? It seems all the more likely from an etymological viewpoint, since those early converts, the original πρεσβύτεροι, would with the passage of fifteen years have become elders in age as well as in name. It is possible that the use of the term elder may have been considered inappropriate in the beginning days of a particular church's existence, even if it had been thought of, for the simple reason that the older persons in the community would have become Christians simultaneously with those who were younger, and since the more aged would not necessarily have been any more expert or faithful at living the Christian life than the young, the leader, old or young, was not chosen for his age but for his fidelity and *longevity in the faith*.[102] To call him an elder when there were many older than he may have seemed awkward, even though the term elder is quite traditional in the Jewish community for example.[103] As time passed, however, such differences between the young and old would have subsided, and the term πρεσβύτερος would then have been able to be used more generally to designate the leaders in the community. In any case, it is clear that by the time Acts is written the term is quite common. The point here is that, while πρεσβύτερος may not have been used in the fifties, there is evidence of emerging Christian leadership by then, and so its

101 Kummel, *op. cit.*, p. 279.

102 For a lucid and plausible explanation of this, and in particular of Stephanas as *presbyteros*, see J. Elliott, *A Home for the Homeless*, pp. 190ff. Cf. above pp. 40–41.

103 Cf. G. Bornkamm, ΠΡΕΣΒΥΣ, in *TDNT*, vol. 6, pp. 651ff.; on the specific question of the Jewish elder, Bornkamm notes, "Instructive, if not uncontested historically is the phrase, 'the elders of Israel' (Exodus 3:16; 12:21; 18:12; 24:1, 9 etc.) which presupposes the unity of the people even before the conquest. Instructive too is the unmistakable tendency to set the established authority of the elders, which needs neither validation nor legal definition, in the service of the guidance of the whole people. Naturally, not all the elders shared in this, but only those chosen by Moses (Numbers 11:16ff). Moses appointed 70 elders at the command of Yahweh." All of this only strengthens the view that structure is *not* a late development in Christianity since Christianity developed organically from the Hebrew people, the existence of whose structured community is beyond doubt. Cf. 1 Timothy 4:12.

use in a Christian work produced in circa AD 70 should not strike us as impossible, or even improbable.

The passage of time from the middle-fifties, when 1 Corinthians was probably written, and AD 70, when this thesis would like to claim 1 Clement was written, was an important fifteen years for the Church. Not only were the individual Churches growing and thus needing more and more guidance, so also were the individual communities multiplying with the result that the Apostle had less and less time and energy to spend on each one. This in turn must have generated the need for further designation of leaders. This is the crucial point: is it so that Paul designated persons as presbyters or not? We have already seen that there are elements in his epistles which show his clear interest in church order and we have even seen him designate Stephanas in Corinth as a leader of some type. But how can we be sure this leader became, with the passage of time, but more importantly with Paul's *explicit* designation, the πρεσβύτερος of which 1 Clement speaks so much?

Perhaps 1 Clement itself can be used to shed some light on this question. Even if we presume that he wrote in the nineties, there can be no question that his mission was a very delicate and difficult one. In effect he was asking for a full retraction of the Corinthians' position and the reinstatement of the ousted presbyters.

In the course of the development of his argument, 1 Clement makes an explicit assertion. In 44:3, which in some ways is the topic sentence of the entire letter, 1 Clement says:

> We consider therefore that it is not just to remove from their ministry those who were appointed by them . . .

By "them," 1 Clement certainly means that some of the presbyters who have been ousted were appointed by the Apostles. This aspect has often been brought up in the context of dating the epistle, as we saw above. But here, entirely apart from the dating question, we have the statement by 1 Clement that the Apostles did in fact appoint presbyters. Naturally, any and every statement cannot be taken for its historical face value, but there seems to be an added reason why this particular assertion of 1 Clement's may be allowed to stand.

The issue is this: if 1 Clement asserted something that either had never been asserted before or which, worse, was not even asserted in Corinth and was demonstrably untrue, his entire argument would have collapsed. It is difficult to believe that the detail that these presbyters had been appointed by the Apostles was something invented by 1 Clement. But neither is it a mere tradition to which 1 Clement is witnessing, in the sense that he really did *think* they were appointed by the Apostles, but wasn't certain. It is much more plausible to believe that here we have a statement about which 1 Clement *was* certain and which he would otherwise never have made. The last thing in the world he would have done, in his position, would have been to make a statement which could have been denied by the rebellious Corinthians. It was because this assertion could not have been denied, i.e. that it *was* a fact, that 1 Clement's argument remained coherent and ultimately prevailed.

Thus, the idea that prior to AD 70 there were presbyters being appointed by the Apostles is not an absurdity. Therefore, there is nothing in 1 Clement's interest in presbyters which would prevent its composition being dated in circa AD 70.

2.1.G *Eschatology*

Another aspect of New Testament thought which must be mentioned in connection with any attempt to establish the dating of 1 Clement is the issue of what has come to be called eschatology. In some ways, this dimension of the New Testament is the most complex and difficult, and in the minds of many, the most important.

A common view is that the earliest stratum of the New Testament shows that the primitive Church expected Jesus to return in a "second coming" and that this was held to be going to occur very soon. With the passage of time, and the dawning realization that the second coming was not to be so imminent after all, Church leadership revised the primitive kerygma and turned their attention to organizational concerns, previously unattended to, in an effort to preserve the movement.[104]

104 I can find no clearer statement of this than that of E. Kasemann, "Paul and Early Catholicism", in *New Testament Questions of Today*, 236–251: "Ever since the eschatological understanding of the New Testament replaced the idealistic interpretation, we can and must determine the various phases of earliest Christian history by means of the original imminent expectation of the parousia, its modifications and its final extinction. Early Catholicism means that transition from earliest Christianity to the so-called ancient Church, which is completed with the disappearance of the imminent expectation." On this point, J. Ratzinger in *Eschatologie*, p. 91, has several important observations to make: "Eine geradlinige Entwicklung in Sachen Naherwar-Lung gibt es nicht. Die Zeit hat, je nach Umständen, die temporale Spannung verschärft oder gedämpft. Zugespitzte zeitliche Erwartung kann unter Umständen gerade auch das Produkt von Rejudaisierung sein, denn das Judentum der Zeit Jesu kennt massive Naherwartungen, die insofern auch rein als solche gar nicht das Besondere Jesu sein können. Das Schema geradliniger Entwicklung ist irreal, der Faktor der angehenden Geschichte bietet keine eindeutigen Urteilsmaßstäbe. Die Naheseschatologie kann gerade auch das Spate sein." That 1 Clement was familiar with *both* Hellenistic and Hebrew culture seems clear. Cf. Jaubert, *op. cit.*, p. 30: "Il faut en effet ou bien le ranger parmi ces familiers de la synagogue hellénistique qu'étaient les craignant Dieu, ou bien admettre qu'il était un juif imprégné de la culture hellénistique de son temps comme tant de juifs de la diaspora." The question of Hellenism vs Judaism in Protochristianity is immense and could well be a thesis topic in itself. J. Daniélou, in a review of O. Knoch's *Eigenwart and Bedeutung der Eschatologie im theologischen Aufriss des ersten Clemensbriefes* [Recherches de Science Rcligieuse 54 (1966), p. 276], says this: "Enfin le livre pose la question fondamentale de la réassomption par le christianisme d'éléments importants de la religiosité hellénistique. Est-ce une trahison par rapport à la pureté du message originel, comme le pensent beaucoup d'historiens du christianisme? Ou est-ce l'expression d'une croissance selon laquelle le christianisme ressaisit les valeurs religieuses pour les sauver, comme je le pence?" Daniélou, then, was inclined to see growth in 1 Clement's Hellenism but in a kind of apologetic effort to preserve the original content of the faith. This is quite different from the simplistic

Now, there can be no doubt that the eschatological aspect of Christianity, i.e. the idea that Jesus would someday return, has never totally been abandoned by Christianity.[105] It remains, for example, an explicit characteristic of liturgical prayer in the Catholic Church. On the other hand, the entire question of eschatology does present a series of substantial *dubia* which the present thesis would hold need to be answered in a manner more accurate than is generally presently the case.

For one thing, the precise meaning of *imminent* or "near" eschatology has to be determined, and, further, it has to be demonstrated where the Christian community expressly held for such a belief as a part of Christian faith. A closer look at the First Letter of Paul to the Thessalonians will illustrate this point.

First Thessalonians has been used as an example of the very earliest stratum of New Testament thought and reflective of this "near" eschatology, the kind presumably abandoned when the original charismatic Church became "catholic." Upon examination, however, 1 Thessalonians can be shown not to hold for all that soon a return of Jesus.[106]

In 4:13, Paul begins the famous section wherein he tries to instruct the Thessalonians on the lot of those who have "fallen asleep." He tells them that they are mistaken in their apparent conclusion that those who survive until the Lord's coming somehow have an advantage over those who have died. He denies that there is any difference between the coming of the Lord for the dead and for the living. All important is the comparison of the day of the Lord, i.e. the day of his return, coming "like a thief in the night." It is to come unexpectedly, suddenly. *"Suddenly" is not the conceptual equivalent of "soon."* Thus it can be said that Paul not only does not reflect a near eschatology, he corrects an overly exact understanding on the part of the Thessalonians that Jesus would return *soon*. This, in a work usually dated as the earliest composed in the New Testament, antedating

theory that 1 Clement is long distant in time as well as in thought from the foundational period of Christianity.

105 One thinks here of the continued use, even in the liturgy, of the Our Father, with its prayer, "Thy kingdom come". Cf. R. Brown, "The Pater Noster as an Eschatological Prayer," in *New Testament Essays*, pp. 275–320. Important too is the Nicene-Constantinople Creed with its two different eschatological affirmations, "*et iterum venturus est cum gloria, iudicare vivos et mortuos*" and "*et expecto resurrectionem mortuorum et vitam venturi saeculi.*" The contemporary and enduring eschatological belief of the Catholic Church is also eloquently expressed in the Second Vatican Council's *Gaudium et Spes* (December 7, 1965), no.39: "We know neither the moment of the consummation of the earth and of man nor the way the universe will be transformed. The form of this world, distorted by sin, is passing away and we are taught that God is preparing a new dwelling and a new earth in which righteousness dwells, whose happiness will fill and surpass all the desires of peace arising in the hearts of men."

106 Even Kummel, *op. cit.*, p. 260, distinguishes between what was the Thessalonians' view and Paul's own: "Evident here (in 1 Thessalonians) is the difficulty into which the former pagans had fallen through the preaching of the imminent eschatological glory (cf. 4:11ff., 1:5:1ff, 14), but also the necessity of bringing into vital harmony the still future responsibility before God and sober moral obligations in the present (5:6ff; 4:3ff; 5:12f, 190)."

all others including the Gospel of Mark with its eschatological expressions which have been interpreted by some as meaning that Jesus himself expected an early eschaton.[107] Since 1 Thessalonians *does* show evidence of a near eschatology *on the part of some* in the local church, but *likewise* shows that Paul himself endeavored to correct what appeared to be a false understanding of the second coming of Jesus, the unconditioned use of near eschatology in a work as a criterion for dating needs to be re-examined.

Why eschatological expectation has been so exaggerated as a sure indication of originality is uncertain. Perhaps it is because Protestant scholars began to observe that their own churches no longer placed upon an imminent return of Jesus the importance that some in the New Testament had given it.[108] Wishing to restore what they believed to be a more original and therefore more authentic Christian belief, they then questioned why it had been abandoned in the first place. They then perhaps concluded that it was the failure of the early prophecies of an imminent second coming combined with a distortion of the original kerygma by a novel interest in structural concerns which explains how the contemporary and

107 Cf. W. G. Kummel, *Promise and Fulfilment: The Eschatological Message of Jesus, passim*, esp. p. 87: "... all these texts confirm that Jesus did indeed count on a shorter or longer period between his death and the parousia, but that he equally certainly proclaimed the threatening approach of the Kingdom of God within his generation." For a Roman Catholic exegete, the situation does not appear quite so clear: R. Brown, *Jesus God and Man*, p. 79: "because there is evidence, nay even a statement, that Jesus did not know when the ultimate victory would take place (Mark 13:32), many Catholic theologians would propose that such knowledge was not an essential of Jesus' mission. Could theologians then also admit that Jesus was not protected from the confused views of his era about the time of the Parousia? An exegete cannot solve such a question; he can only point out the undeniable confusion in the statements attributed to Jesus."

108 The Protestant positions are, of course, varied and nuanced as Kummel, ibid., points out at length. For the precise meaning of imminent eschatology in the contemporary context, note what Hummel says, p. 152: "If therefore the *imminent* expectation, being a necessary contemporary form of expression can certainly be detached from Jesus' message, the future expectation is essential and indispensable, because in this form alone can the nature of God's redemptive action *in history* be held fast." John H. Elliott, in "A Catholic Gospel: Reflections on Early Catholicism in the New Testament," p. 214, summarizes the "early catholic" movement in Protestant scholarship: "With the sobriquet 'early catholic' are identified Christian documents ante-dating the emergence of the 'Great' or 'catholic' Church ca. 180 A.D., which show traces of or tendencies in the direction of, the following: the organization of the Church according to hierarchical in contrast to charismatic ministry; the development of the monarchical episcopate; an objectification of the proclamation and an emphasis upon a strictly formulated rule of faith; a stress upon 'orthodoxy' or 'sound doctrine' in opposition to false teaching; moralization of the faith and conception of the gospel as new law; an objective understanding of the faith in objective rather than subjective, in static rather than dynamic terms, as *fides quae creditur* in contrast to *fides qua creditur*; a development of the principle of apostolic succession and transmitted authority; a distinction between laity and clergy; a conception of an authoritative interpretation of the scriptures; a trend toward 'sacramentalism'; the formulation of a natural theology; a concern for ecclesiastical unity and consolidation; and an interest in the collecting of apostolic writings." Joseph Fitzmyer in *The Gospel According to Luke* I–IX, p. 23, identifies Ernst Troeltsch (1865–1923) as the first to use the term, originally as a *terminus technicus* in sociology.

presumably less authentic Christian church experience evolved. We have already seen that the thesis that there was at any time a structureless, charismatic period in the Church should have to be proven, not simply asserted.

Also, since the earliest records we have of Christianity are the Pauline epistles and they can be shown to have clear signs of a lively interest in structure, the case for the existence of a purely charismatic Christian church is seriously challenged. If it is objected that certain passages in the Synoptics and in Paul would seem to reflect an imminent eschatology, then that very fact would seem to demonstrate that imminent eschatology *and* a structured church *can* co-exist since, by all modern historical critical criteria for interpretation of the gospel material, the gospels themselves were written in their final form in a Church setting (*Sitz im Leben der Kirche*).

It cannot be pretended that this is a sufficient examination of the entire issue of New Testament eschatology. It is only intended to raise a serious doubt regarding whether eschatology in and of itself can be considered a reliable indication of dating. The doubt only increases when the eschatological perspective of 1 Clement itself is examined.

In 1 Clement 21:9, it states, "... his breath is in us, and when he will he shall take it away."

> 23:5: "Truly his will shall be quickly and suddenly (ταχὺ καὶ ἐξαίφνης) accomplished," as the Scripture also bears witness that "he shall come quickly and will not tarry; and the Lord shall suddenly come to his Temple, and the Holy One for whom ye look."
>
> 24:1: ... the Master continually proves to us that there will be a future resurrection ...
>
> 27:5: ... when he will and as he will he will do all things ...
>
> 28:1: ... that we may be sheltered from the judgments to come.
>
> 42:3: ... they went forth, in the assurance of the Holy Spirit preaching the Good News that the Kingdom of God is coming.

Particularly interesting from the point of view both of the eschatology involved and the dating of the letter, is the expression of the plan of the Apostles for their successors in 44:2:

> For this cause, therefore, since they had received perfect foreknowledge, they appointed those who have already been mentioned, and afterward added the codicil that if they should fall asleep (ἐάν κοιμηθῶσιν) other approved men should succeed to their ministry.

A temporal clause when it expresses a time which is future in relation to the time of the main verb may be expressed with the subjunctive with ἐάν, or with ὅταν. The fact that the author chose ἐάν is not necessarily an indication that he meant the clause to be conditional (although Lake takes it as such above). Still, it *may* be conditional and if so, the intriguing question arises whether or not this is such an early text that the author, who may have known the Apostles personally, is indicating that there actually had been a time when there was some doubt that they would die before the second coming.[109]

> 50:3: ... a place among the pious who shall be made manifest at
> the visitation of the Kingdom of Christ."

Then, in v. 4, 1 Clement quotes Isaiah 26:20: "For it is written, enter into thy chambers for a very little while (μικρὸν ὅσον ὅσον) until my wrath and fury pass away ..."

Taken as a whole, the above would seem to indicate that, whenever it was written, 1 Clement still nurtures the eschatological expectation of the second coming of Christ, and even that it would occur *soon*. As should be clear from the above, much still needs to be clarified about the whole issue of New Testament eschatology especially as regards dating, but from these texts of 1 Clement it is clear that he does have an evident, if not overly precise, understanding that the return of the Lord was still expected in his day. *But, even if 1 Clement were written in the nineties*, such an eschatological perspective is not what we are led to expect in any work dated so late. According to those who would see eschatology as a sure indication of date, such texts as these amount to practical proof that 1 Clement is early, not late. The least that can be said is that, like Paul, 1 Clement shows an intense eschatological interest side by side with a concern for church order. After all, church order is the point of the entire letter!

2.1.H *Apostolic Succession*

One of the principal dogmatic points to be found in 1 Clement, as is widely recognized, is the doctrine of the apostolic succession. Some have accused 1 Clement, understood as written in 96, of having invented the teaching. It is true that apostolic *succession* in the sense of a second generation of church leaders taking the place of the Apostles is not explicitly to be found in the New Testament. On the other hand, it is far from true that the doctrine has no New Testament roots or parallels. Just a few will be noted here.

In Galatians Paul forcefully defends his gospel, that is, not *his* gospel, but the one he was preaching. The distinction is important because it helps show that Paul was defending himself against those who were charging him with not preaching the real gospel, but one which came "from men." In 1:11 he writes:

109 Cf. John 21:23.

> For I would have you know, brethren, that the gospel which was preached by me is not man's gospel. For I did not receive it from man, nor was I taught it, but it came through a revelation of Jesus Christ.

Nevertheless in 2:2, still by a "revelation," Paul relates that he went up to Jerusalem and laid before "those who were of repute" (later, in 2:9, identified as James, Cephas, and John) the gospel as he had preached it to the Gentiles, "lest somehow I should be running or had run in vain." In 1:1ff., Paul gives his famous account of how he had had to oppose Cephas to his face over the question of the permissibility of Christian Jews to share table fellowship with Gentile converts. Throughout the episode Paul stresses, by implication, the importance he saw in convincing Cephas of his view. It is as though Paul recognized that if he lost this battle to Cephas, then it would be a fatal loss, since Cephas was one of those "in repute," which is to say, the Apostles. Paul had already stressed the importance he laid on apostleship in Galatians 1:1: "Paul an apostle—not from men nor through man, but through Jesus Christ and God the Father." In what follows, Paul admits, as it were, that he had even gone to Jerusalem and compared his gospel with that of the "pillars" and had had the hand of fellowship, of approval, extended to him by the Apostles. He opposes one of these Apostles when he is convinced that Cephas was not being "straightforward about the truth of the Gospel." It is important to realize that this presentation was being made, in context, for the good of the Galatian Christians who were themselves being tempted to believe "another gospel" (v. 69). Thus Paul reflects two essential things: that the gospel does not originate with men, not even with the Apostles (!), but also that the true gospel is authenticated by the witness of the Apostles, hence the fierce opposition to Cephas' error. We can begin to see, then, that the apostolic stamp of approval was already a value for Paul.

In another context Paul also admits that, at least in its particular details, he, too, had "received" the gospel. Reference is made to the extremely important, and ancient formulation of the content of the kerygma in 1 Corinthians 15:1–11. In this section, Paul stresses the importance of the gospel, that it precedes the Apostles, but in its being revealed to them, they become its witnesses:

> 5. ... and that he appeared to Cephas and then to the twelve. ... 7. Then he appeared to James and then to all the apostles. 8. Last of all, as to one untimely born, he appeared also to me. ... 11. Whether then it was I or they, so we preach and so you believed.

Here we have Paul's doctrine that the gospel comes from God but through the Apostles, himself among them. His own dependence on the preaching of the Apostles is with regard to the details of the content, that Christ died for our sins, and that he was buried and that he was raised on the third day, in accordance with the Scriptures. But for the power of the gospel itself, he depends on no one, having received a vision of the Risen Lord himself, whence derives his apostleship. But what is essential here is that Paul links the preaching of the gospel to the Apostles: it is they, and he of course, who preach the gospel. Thus, again, we have Paul himself forging the all-important link between the gospel's authenticity and the person of the Apostles. This tradition, especially later in times of persecution and heretical division in Christianity, would give the apostolic character of the gospel new significance and the apostolic origin of Church leadership a new urgency. Finally, it would become the hallmark par excellence of the orthodox gospel.[110] 1 Clement is a stage in the lengthy development of a full-blown doctrine of apostolic succession, but he can by no means be said to have created it *ex nihilo* if, as we have seen, the apostolic character of the gospel itself was already so essential in the mind of Paul.

2.1.I Summary

To summarize this entire section, the following points seem clear enough:

1. Dependence of 1 Clement on the New Testament has to be shown and not simply asserted. If, as appears increasingly probable, 1 Clement was written in circa AD 70, it is not probable that he would have yet had access to a collection of Pauline letters. In any case, attempts to show dependence of 1 Clement on individual Pauline compositions by showing similarity between isolated phrases are undermined by that very questionable method.

2. Nevertheless, 1 Clement can be shown to reflect what might be described as a primitive theological viewpoint. This is especially true of his neglect of any anti-Temple polemic, his familiarity with the "Suffering Servant" theme, his naming of only two Apostles, and his fluid terminology, referring interchangeably to ἐπίσκοποι and πρεσβύτεροι.

3. When compared more thematically with Paul, 1 Clement shows a similar understanding of Church order and eschatology. There are scant grounds for the generalization that near eschatology is original and incompatible with an interest in Church structure. First Clement shows evidence of an eschatology every bit as "imminent" as Paul's, and again like Paul, has a substantial concern for Church unity and order.

4. All in all, there is little in the New Testament which would preclude an earlier dating for 1 Clement and there are several elements which would seem to favor it.

2.2 The Apostolic Fathers

Keeping in mind our primary interest in determining the most probable date of 1 Clement, it will be likewise helpful, in addition to showing 1 Clements relationship

110 For a succinct view of this later perspective, see J. Ratzinger, "Primacy, Episcopate and Apostolic Succession" in H. Rahner and J. Ratzinger, *The Episcopate and the Primacy*, esp. pp. 55ff.

or lack of it to the New Testament, to say something about the *Sitz im Leben* of 1 Clement as compared to the other non-scriptural Christian works of the first or second centuries. The works which will concern us here are the *Didache* and the seven epistles of Ignatius of Antioch.

2.2.A *The Didache*

The complicated textual history of the *Didache*, or the "Teaching of the Twelve Apostles", makes the determination of the original recension of it conjectural at best, and the certain dating of that recension practically impossible. A scholarly consensus has nevertheless been that it probably dates from the early second century, or possibly earlier.[111] The *Didache* does give us some idea of the state of church order at the time in the community in which it was written, but unfortunately we are not able to say with any degree of certainty where the document originated or who its intended recipients were. If we did know, it would be invaluable to show the development of church order in those areas since the *Didache* is markedly different from both 1 Clement and the epistles of Ignatius.

It seems to be addressed not to leaders of a Christian community, but to the community at large (it lacks a specific introduction). Its topics are wide-ranging and would apply to everyone. Leaders are never addressed as such.

The Church in the *Didache* is conceived of in very general terms: 10:5:

> Remember, Lord, thy Church, to deliver it from all evil, and to make it perfect in thy love, and gather it together in its holiness from the four winds to thy kingdom which thou hast prepared for it.

This global or "great" church perspective is a much belabored one, but there does seem to be reason to see it as a result of a later theological perspective. As we shall see below, it is not until Ignatius of Antioch (whose dates in the early first century seem a matter of general consensus) that we meet the explicit formulation, "the catholic (καθολική) church."[112] Whatever the case, the terminology in 1 Clement does not reflect this "great church" usage, but is uniform in its reference to the *local* church:

> Introduction: The Church of God which sojourns in Rome to the Church of God which sojourns in Corinth
>
> 44:3: We consider therefore that it is not just to remove from their ministry those who were appointed by them, or later

111 The scholarly divisions on the issue of the date and the provenance of the Didache are so wide that one guess literally seems as good as another. For a brief summary of the contemporary situation, see Brown and Meier, *Antioch and Rome*, p. 81, esp. no. 180.

112 To the Smyrnaeans 8:2; cf. also Brown and Meier, *op. cit.*, p. 78 *et passim*.

on by other eminent men, with the consent of the whole Church (συνευδοκησάσης τῆς ἐκκλησίας πάσης).

47:6: The steadfast and ancient church of the Corinthians is being disloyal to the presbyters.

If the local church emphasis can be viewed as the earlier, 1 Clement's ecclesiology might justifiably be seen as representing a period prior to the emergence of the explicit "great Church" consciousness seen in the *Didache*.

As regards church structure specifically, the *Didache* seems to recognize a terminology of teachers, Apostles and Prophets as titles for itinerant Christian teachers, a language that 1 Clement does not share at all. In chapter 11 we find:

> Whoever then comes and teaches you all these things aforesaid, receive him. But if the teacher himself be perverted and teach another doctrine, do not listen to him. ... And concerning the Apostles and Prophets. ... Let every Apostle who comes to you be received as the Lord, but let him not stay more than one day or if need be a second as well: but if he stay three days he is a false prophet. And when an Apostle goes forth let him accept nothing but bread ... but if he ask for money, he is a false prophet. Do not test or examine any prophet who is speaking in a spirit. ... But not everyone who speaks in a spirit is a prophet, except he have the behavior of the Lord. From his behavior, then, the false prophet and the true prophet shall be known.

In addition to these itinerant figures, the *Didache* also shows acceptance of the bishop/deacon bi-partite hierarchy, 15:1ff:

> Appoint therefore for yourselves bishops and deacons worthy of the Lord, meek men, and not lovers of money, and truthful and approved, for they also minister to you the ministry of the prophets and the teachers. Therefore do not despise them for they are your honorable men, together with the prophets and teachers.

The word for appoint is χειροτονήσατε, etymologically related to χείρ, or hand. The term is used twice in the New Testament, once in Acts 14:23:

> and when they had appointed elders for them χειροτονήσαντες δὲ αὐτοῖς in every church ...

and in 2 Corinthians 8:19:

> He has been appointed by the churches to travel with us ...
> (χειροτονηθεὶς ὑπὸ τῶν ἐκκλησιῶν).

The term does not appear in the LXX or in any other Greek versions of the Old Testament, nor in the so-called Apocrypha. In the later patristic period, however, the term will be used of imperial appointments as well as of ordinations by imposition of hands.[113] Whether the etymology reflects an explicit and conscious reference to imposition of hands in the *Didache*, we cannot know. In any case, the word is absent from 1 Clement who knows nothing of the imposition of hands. When he speaks of appointment, e.g. 44:3, he uses καθίστημι "those who were appointed by them (κατασταθέντας ὑπ᾽ ἐκείνων)." The point here is that *if* the word implies imposition of hands, to whose hands is the *Didache* referring? It does not say. It does seem to imply, though, a situation in which the author, while recognizing the common practice of welcoming itinerant preachers, seems to be preferring the residential structure of church leaders as we find in 1 Clement. At first sight this period of flux, or transition from itinerant to residential leaders, may seem to be the more ancient, but further analysis may not support that view. For example, the "Apostles" referred to in the *Didache* bear no resemblance to the Apostles mentioned in 1 Clement or in the Synoptics. That is, they are probably not the original Apostles, like Peter and Paul, or the Twelve, but reminiscent of the Apostles mentioned in Ephesians 4:11:

> And his gifts were that some should be apostles, some prophets,
> some evangelists, some pastors and teachers

in which it appears that the church order is quite pluriform.

Further, the *Didache* shows concern over the *false* Apostle and prophet, hardly one of the originals! This suggests that after the period of the original Apostles, the title was maintained in some kind of honorific way, and given to those who claimed it. It also suggests a considerable amount of deceit on the part of charlatans, against whom the community now needs to be put on guard. It is thus a *later* development.

First Clement shows no such complications. If anything, he is remarkable in the fact that he does not even leave room in his analysis of the Corinthians' dispute for the possibility that the presbyters themselves may have been at least in part responsible for the subsequent complete rupture. He may have known some of them personally, although we cannot be sure of this. In any case, the fact that 1 Clement is a) not aware of any other structure, such as itinerants, prophets, and teachers etc., and b) that he has not yet had the experience, later to become so sadly common, of errant clergy, seems to suggest at least the possibility of an earlier date.

---

113 Cf. G. W. H. Lampe, *A Patristic Greek Lexicon*, CHEIROTONEO, pp. 1522–1523.

2.2.B The Epistles of Ignatius

It is in Ignatius of Antioch in his several extant letters[114] that we see most clearly an early defense of a tri-partite hierarchy, single-bishop, priests, and deacons, a structure which will later become universal in the Church and undisputed until the sixteenth-century.

In his Epistle to the Smyrneans, Ignatius reflects his characteristic insistence on the monepiscopal structure:

> 8:1: See that you all follow the bishop, as Jesus Christ follows the Father. ... Let no one do any of the things appertaining to the Church without the bishop. ... Let that be considered a valid Eucharist which is celebrated by the bishop, or by one whom he appoints. It is not lawful to baptise or to hold an agape without the bishop: but whatever he approve, this is also pleasing to God, that everything which you do may be secure and valid.

This is of key importance since Ignatius nowhere shows that he knows who the bishop of Smyrna is but clearly assumes that there is one: 12:2: "I salute the godly bishop, and the revered presbytery." In the introduction to his letter, where Ignatius would have normally named the bishop had he known him, he does not do so but addresses the epistle "to the Church of God ... which is in Smyrna in Asia." In turn, this becomes important when it is recalled that when he writes to the Romans, he likewise omits reference to the local bishop, leading some to infer that this omission is proof that the monepiscopal structure had not yet emerged at Rome. Such was clearly *not* the case when he wrote to Smyrna, since he emphasized the role of the single bishop though he fails to mention him by name. We should take Ignatius at his word when he writes to the Trallians, 3:1: "without the deacon, presbyter and bishop, the name of Church is not given."[115] When he writes to the Romans, nevertheless, not only does he address them as a church, but describes this church as the "Church beloved and enlightened ... which has the presidency in the country of the Romans, worthy of God, worthy in its holiness, and pre-eminent in love" and in 3:1: "You never have envied anyone, you taught oth-

114 For a full treatment of the scholarly state of the question regarding the authenticity of the seven letters of Ignatius, see W. Schoedel, "Are the Letters of Ignatius of Antioch Authentic?", in *Religious Studies Review* 6 (1980), 196–201. The purpose of the present study is not to inquire whether or not the letters are authentic (it presupposes that they are), but whether, if they arc authentic and to be dated in ca. AD 108–117, there is anything in them which would militate against the thesis that 1 Clement was written in ca. AD 70. Cf. also P. Th. Camelot, *Lettres d'Ignace d'Antioche*, 13–16.

115 Cf. W. R. Schoedel, *Ignatius of Antioch, A Commentary on the Letters*, 145: "... here he (Ignatius) is explicit in recognizing no Church without all three (orders). He must have found them in place wherever he went to make this statement in the matter of fact way he does."

ers." Still, Ignatius knows that they know what a bishop is, in 2:2, he writes: "You may sing to the Father in Christ Jesus, that God has vouchsafed that the bishop of Syria shall be found at the setting of the sun." Therefore, if Ignatius can use the term bishop and be confident that he will be understood, and if he says that he would not give the title church to any community without a bishop, and if he not only calls the Roman community a church, but praises it lavishly, it seems to follow that there was indeed a monepiscopal structure customary by that time in Rome. Why Ignatius did not name the bishop, here or in the letter to the Smyrneans, we do not know. He may have heard that the bishop had died and did not yet know who had replaced him. The fact that he thinks that there was not *presently* an officially recognized bishop may have even been the reason for his letter since he is afraid that the Romans might for some reason interfere with his being martyred. Perhaps he thought this was more of a possibility since they had not yet decided on their new bishop. Or again, he may not have wanted to guess, or make a mistake about the bishop's name, which would clearly have been a *faux pas*. In any case, to claim that from a mere omission of the bishop's name one might validly deduce that Ignatius was prepared to make an exception to his rule that every church, to be a church, had to have a bishop, is exaggerated.

How does this relate to 1 Clement? Robinson argues that, if 1 Clement with its bi-partite hierarchy, is dated in AD 96, this would leave little time before Ignatius, writing in the teens of the first century, who describes single bishops and a tri-partite structure. He observes reasonably, "If this is really the state of affairs in Rome in 96, then we are faced with a very remarkable transition within less than twenty years to that presupposed by the epistles of Ignatius. For he, while addressing the church of Rome in the salutation of his epistle to it with the utmost veneration, says elsewhere that apart from the three orders of bishop, presbyters and deacons 'there is not even the name of a church' (Trallians 3), and he speaks of bishops, in this sense, as being by then 'settled in the farthest parts of the earth' (Ephesians 3; cf. Ephesians 4ff.; Magnesians 3:6ff.; Trallians 2ff.; Philadelphians 4; Smyrnaeans 8). It is easier to believe that 1 Clement ... reflects an earlier period."[116]

On one hand, the fact that Ignatius does make it so explicit that by his day single bishops had been appointed everywhere (*οἱ ἐπίσκοποι οἱ κατὰ τὰ πέρατα ὁρισθέντες*, Ephesians 3:2) has not generally been given much consideration in contemporary scholarship. On the other hand, though, it should be admitted that Robinson does seem to reflect the presumption that the hierarchical structure within the ancient Church developed along somewhat straight and identical lines which continue to the present day. Modern scholars (but dating back well into the 19th century) would insist that the pluralism of the early Church be recognized as applying not only to doctrine (orthodoxy vs. heresy) but also to the form in which the individual local church was organized. Thus, there is nothing

116 Robinson, *op. cit.*, 328.

per se to have prevented Ignatius from insisting on a monepiscopal structure in all the eastern churches over which he had some influence, while in the church at Rome, whom he explicitly declines to instruct (see Romans 4:3), the bipartite (presbyter-deacon) structure endured. According to this view, Ignatius would have been exaggerating in his claim that single bishops had been appointed "to the ends of the earth." Likewise, his silence in his letter to the Romans about a monarchical bishop *may* indicate that there was not one there yet.[117] *If* this were *proven* to be the case, Robinson's argument about the small time allowed for the development of the single episcopate at Rome after 1 Clement but before Ignatius would no longer be valid. Nevertheless, and this needs to be emphasized even at the risk of irritating repetition, if there was not monepiscopacy at Rome, even by the time of Ignatius, *all the more reason* why the classical date of AD 96 for 1 Clement has to be reconsidered since it depends on the presumption that there *was* a monepiscopate at Rome when 1 Clement was written, because it is about this monepiscopacy that Eusebius wrote, from whom we get the AD 96 date in the first place! Since 1 Clement is not a monepiscopal letter, the existence of monepiscopacy at Rome in AD 96 is not directly relevant to establishing its most probable date. On the other hand, the assertion that there was *not* monepiscopacy at Rome before Ignatius, while not without its problems, is not compatible with the majority opinion in favor of the AD 96 fixing.

Through all of this, whether one is researching the date of 1 Clement or the monepiscopacy at Rome in the first century, several cautions should be kept in mind. First of all, it has to be recalled how very sparse is the actual data we have today which can with certainty be dated to the first century and which explicitly refers to the state of the small and far-flung Christian communities. When one adds to this the fact that these churches were subject to harassment both from the side of the Jews who resented its development as a sect within Judaism, and from the part of the Romans who, especially under Nero, had not extended to the Roman Christians their traditional policy of religious toleration, one begins to see that the lack of much hard and fast historical data is not surprising. But it is the lack of this data which makes a broad-based scientifically historical study practically impossible. All of this renders the study of the date of 1 Clement more and more important. Because we can concentrate here on internal as well as external evidence to establish it, the date of 1 Clement may indeed serve to stabilize, at least as regards the Roman and Corinthian communities, our chronicle of developments

117 So, Brown in Brown and Meier, *op. cit.*, 163; "Indeed the signal failure of Ignatius (ca. 110) to mention the single-bishop in his letter to the Romans (a very prominent theme in his other letters), and the usage of Hermas, which speaks of plural presbyters (Vis. 2.4.2.) and bishops (Sim. 9.27.2), make it likely that the single bishop structure did not come to Rome till ca. 140–150." Also, P. Lampe in *op. cit.* esp. pp. 334ff. L. comes to substantially the same conclusion but dates the emergence of the monepiscopate at Rome even later: "Die Fraktionierung in Rom begunstigte eine kollegiale Presbyterialverfassung and behinderte langer—bis zur zweiten Halfte des 2. Jh.—die Ausbildung eines monarchischen Episkopates in der Stadt."

in the palaeochristian period. The irony has been that among church historians, biblicists, and systematic theologians, the *value* of a clear date for 1 Clement was never in doubt. The present study merely wishes to raise some serious doubts about the *certitude* with which the received date of 1 Clement has been held, and to suggest an alternative date on a more objective basis.

Maintaining our focus on the issue of the probable amount of time which lapsed between the writing of 1 Clement and the Ignatian epistles, and the implications that time may have for the dating of 1 Clement, there are two other questions which should be treated here.

The first is Ignatius' attitude toward Judaism. Even in his day, long after the destruction of the Temple and the publication of the famous Sixteenth Benediction which the rabbis wrote to excommunicate Christians who still clung to their Jewish origins,[118] Ignatius indicates that for him the continued practice of Judaism by a convert Christian is unacceptable as well:

> For if we are living until now according to Judaism, we confess that we have not received grace (Magnesians 8:1).

And again in 10:3: "It is monstrous to talk of Jesus Christ and to practice Judaism."

And in the letter to the Philippians: "But if anyone interpret Judaism to you do not listen to him" (Philadelphians 6:1).

This is in marked contrast with the benign manner of 1 Clement who can still speak of the Temple, its priests, and sacrifices with a praise that shows that he believes that this central aspect of Judaism is nothing other than God's will. Even if one were to insist that 1 Clement is looking back toward the Temple of former days, his religious nostalgia for Judaism is simply not that of Ignatius. A fair explanation of the divergence seems to be that their entire situations are changed: If 1 Clement was written when the Temple was still standing, the continued use of it by Christian converts from Judaism would not seem surprising, and hence 1 Clement's favorable references. On the other hand, Ignatius in his day faced a situation where not only had Judaism been shown to belong to the former Covenant, but Christians were expelled from Jewish synagogues and the difference between Christian and Jew was seen as increasingly acute. Ignatius' attitude is understandable since he wrote in the early years of the second century. But the same reasons which make Ignatius' approach seem natural would also have prevailed in the last decade of the first century, after the anti-Christian policies had been formulated in Jamnia in circa 90. Thus, 1 Clement again seems to come from an earlier era.

Another issue in Ignatius which invites attention is his eschatology. In the Epistle to the Ephesians, chap. 6, he writes:

118 For further treatment of the Sixteenth Benediction, see R. Brown, *The Community of the Beloved Disciple*, 22.

> These are the last times. Therefore let us be modest, let us fear the long suffering of God that it may not become our judgment.

In the Epistle to the Smyrneans, chap. 9:1, he writes:

> Moreover, it is reasonable for us to return to soberness, while we still have time to repent towards God.

He will frequently call Jesus, our "hope" and he refers often to being "found," eg. Ephesians 10:3: "that no plant of the devil be found in you but that you remain in all purity."

The reason for mentioning this is again the theory that the eschatological dimension, especially as characterized by the expectation of the "near" parousia, is a characteristic of *early* Christian belief, which dissipated with the passage of time, i.e. when it was obvious that the second coming of Jesus was not going to be so "imminent" after all. As we saw above, the standard characterization of the imminent eschaton as the hallmark of the original kerygma, which then was revised in light of the apparent postponement of the second coming, is a dangerously simplistic analysis and a reductionist "collapsing" of the manifold elements of the kerygma into only one of its dimensions. Ignatius, while he cannot be said to be fixated on the eschatological elements, clearly maintains an eschatological dimension to his thought, as the Christian Church always would. *Exactly* how near this eschaton was believed to be, is not possible to *certify*. That Ignatius in the early years of the second century believed he was still living in "the last times" despite the passage of "time," seems clear from the passages just cited.

2.2.C *Summary*

To summarize this material on the *Didache* and Ignatius, then, it can be said that 1 Clement appears to come from an earlier period. He knows nothing of the complications facing the recipients of the didactic nor does he reflect a knowledge of the fully-developed monepiscopate either at Rome or at Corinth. All of this makes an earlier dating hypothesis more attractive.

In general, then, from our examination of the New Testament and other early Christian literature, 1 Clement can be shown to contain numerous elements which reflect a generally archaic theological perspective. The presumption that no early Christian work would have an interest in church structure can be seen to be unfounded by the presence already in Paul of pervasive interest in church order and unity. But the bias that any trace of attention to church order is necessarily a sign of a later composition is massive. For the present, suffice it to say that there is nothing in any of the extant early Christian literature which would prevent an early, circa AD 70, dating for 1 Clement, and much that would recommend it.

Chapter 3
Theological Implications of an Earlier Dating Hypothesis

Our task in Chapter One was to set down the principal internal and external evidence for positing an early, circa AD 70 date for 1 Clement. We saw that that evidence is considerable. In chapter two, the newly dated 1 Clement was contrasted with the New Testament, especially the letters of Paul to the Romans and the two to the Corinthians. It was found that there was nothing in Paul, even in the earliest strata of the Pauline literature, which would exclude a circa AD 70 date for 1 Clement. Other early Christian works especially Ignatius of Antioch and the *Didache*, were reviewed and, similarly, they do not seem to contain any material which would prevent a circa AD 70 dating for 1 Clement. There remains for us now to consider, in a somewhat speculative vein, what consequences such an early dating hypothesis would have. This third chapter will take up that question and approach it from two related but distinct perspectives. In a first section, the discussion will center on what possible effects a circa AD 70 date would have for the interpretation of 1 Clement itself. As has already been seen, the present massive scholarly consensus, still in place, for a circa AD 96 date has been the backdrop for nearly all the major commentaries and studies made on 1 Clement. Catholic and Protestant scholars, while perhaps differing on their understanding of the meaning of 1 Clement, have been nevertheless united in their belief that it is to be dated in the middle nineties of the first century. Since in the case of 1 Clement, probably more than in any other document of the early Christian Church, it is its *date* which is a key to its meaning and importance for theology, a change in that date will undoubtedly affect how it is understood. In a second section, the perspective will be widened to sketch out the possible effects of an earlier dating of 1 Clement for theology in general. In neither case can one pretend here to attempt an exhaustive review of the numerous studies of 1 Clement, and nothing more than a brief outline of the specific issues can be proposed. Moreover, it should be clear from the outset that no dating hypothesis, in and of itself, will be conclusive one way or the other for any of the specific problems related to 1 Clement. With these precautions in mind, we can proceed.

3.1 I Clement as Seen from the Perspective of a circa AD 70 Date

3.1.A The Use of the Old Testament in 1 Clement

An early, circa AD 70, date for 1 Clement would help us see him not as a "turn of the century" heir of an already developed Christian exegesis of the Old Testament, but rather as a concrete example of how, prior to the composition and circulation of the canonical gospels, a Christian theologian made agile use of the Hebrew Scriptures. First Clement, whether he was a Gentile conversant with Judaism or a Hellenistic Jewish convert to Christianity, was thoroughly conversant with the Old Testament, as Hagner has amply demonstrated.[119] As a Christian theologian, reflecting on the Old Testament in light of the needs of his contemporary Christian community, 1 Clement draws from them deep insights which would help explain a variety of elements in the Christian religion.[120]

New Testament scholars have long pointed to the reliance of the New Testament on the Hebrew Scriptures, not only demonstrated by the Old Testament quotations, but also by the incorporation into the New Testament of rich symbolic motifs of Old Testament origin. The clearest examples in 1 Clement are perhaps his use of Psalm 22 and Isaiah 53 and his use of the Suffering Servant image. If we understand 1 Clement as written in AD 70, before the composition, or at least the circulation of the Christian Gospels, we can then better appreciate him as one of those theologians whose important work on the Old Testament roots of Christianity helped interpret the new faith to Hebrew and Gentile converts alike and which would later make an important contribution to the composition of the written Gospels. Certainly no rigid time line is being envisioned here between the so-called oral and written stages of Gospel composition. Perhaps Mark had already been written, even though 1 Clement cannot be shown to have known Mark, much less depended on him. Rather, 1 Clement can be seen as an exponent of the need to look to the Old Testament for guidance in the daily life and comportment of the Christian church. His multiple examples of upright behavior drawn from the pages of the Old Testament, and so reminiscent of the hallakic style of his rabbinic counterparts in Judaism, are all signs of a generation of theologians who formed a bridge between the synagogue and the proto-christian church.[121] His positive admiration for the Temple and its sacrifices, the Hebrew distinction between clergy and laity, and the absence of any of the rancour which would later mark the relations between Jews and Christians, especially Christians of Jewish origin, all help locate 1 Clement in the more tranquil era prior to the fall of Jerusalem and its Temple, an event so catastrophic for Judaism, but an era so crucial and productive for Christian theology.[122] This early, even original, tendency of Christian theol-

119 Hagner, *op. cit.*, 21.

120 Ibid., 132: "The choice, the interpretation and the application of Old Testament texts are governed by the urgent necessity of meeting the problems of Corinthian Church. In correction of the scandalous situation at Corinth, Clement skillfully employs the most effective weapon known to him, the direct application of the timeless oracles of God."

121 Ibid., 130: "Despite these examples of allegorization, it must be admitted that Clement's allegorical interpretation is of a rather elementary kind."

122 Much more could be said about 1 Clement's connections to Judaism. Cf. eg. H. Thyen, *Der Stil der Jadisch-Hellenistischen Homelie*, p. 118, "Wie aus solcher jiidischer Homiletik christliche

ogy to look to the Old Testament for help in understanding the true meaning of the Jesus event, helps us appreciate the fact that the Christian regard for the Old Testament, and its ultimate acceptance of it as forming part of the canon, on a par with the Christian Scriptures, is no subsequent development in Christian theology but a given and fundamental tenet of the Christian faith. It is not surprising then to find that contemporary New Testament scriptural studies would hypothesize that, prior to the writing of the Gospels, there had to have been a period in which the Old Testament was reflected upon and particular passages singled out which had a particularly Christian significance. What is somewhat surprising is that, if the circa AD 70 date for 1 Clement were accepted, we would now find in him an instance of those early Christian theologians whose existence, prior to the writing and diffusion of the Gospels, had been presumed to be a fact. With the earlier dating, 1 Clement could be studied now, not as the *product* of the New Testament period, but as a rare, even unique, example of one who made a *contribution* to the writing of the New Testament itself.

3.1.B The New Testament in an Earlier 1 Clement

There are likewise various implications for 1 Clement's use of the New Testament if 1 Clement can be shown to have been written in circa AD 70.

The most obvious implication is that 1 Clement would then be far too early to have known of any "canon" of New Testament writings, or any collections of Pauline writings. Some, especially D. Hagner, have argued *from* a purported knowledge of several Pauline texts *to* 1 Clement's familiarity with a collection of Paul's works, and further concluded that we can with some probability therefore date these collections prior to AD 95, for him, the presumed date of 1 Clement.[123] The issue of whether 1 Clement knew much at all of the writings that later became known as the New Testament was examined above, and it was found that 1 Clement's knowledge of much of the New Testament, with the exceptions of 1 Corinthians, and perhaps Romans and Hebrews, is extremely dubious. It follows that inferences based on an already weak hypothesis are even less probable.

On the other hand, 1 Clement is familiar with two sayings of Jesus that appear, though in a different form, in the Synoptics.[124]

The entire question of the sources of the Synoptics can be raised here since both they and 1 Clement share two versions of two quotations directly attributed by both the Synoptics and 1 Clement to the Lord himself. Do they derive from the famous "Q"? Is 1 Clement a witness to the long hypothesized oral tradition, prior

---

Predigt werden kann, zeigen uns deutlich der Hebrews and der 1 Clement deren Form ganz die der synagogalen Homilie ist" (cited in Fuellenbach, *op. cit.*, p. 170, no. 205). Cf. also J. Daniélou, *Theologie du Judeo-Christianisme*, pp. 53–55.

123 Ibid., 331.

124 1 Clement 13:2 // Matthew 5:7; 6:14; 7:1–2 // Mark 45:24; 11:25. 1 Clement 46:8 // Matthew 26:24; 18:6 // Mark 14:21; 9:42 // Luke 17:2.

to the writing of the Gospels? Were there different written forms of the sayings of Jesus circulating, one used by the gospel writers and one by 1 Clement? Naturally these and other related questions cannot be settled here, but it is important to show that 1 Clement's relationship to the entire question of the Synoptics would be completely revised if he were seen to have been written before them, or before some of them. He would be more readily able to be seen as a witness, though in written form, to a handing down of sayings of the Lord prior to their classical formulation in the Gospels.

As far as the other New Testament materials are concerned, each work would deserve separate treatment, of course, but the possible relationship between individual works of the New Testament and 1 Clement would have to be pursued in a new way if it can now be accepted that 1 Clement may have been written before and not after them. The least that can be said in this regard is that 1 Clement is an important example of the state of Roman theology, with key insights especially in christology and ecclesiology, from the period prior to the destruction of the Jerusalem Temple. That event, again, with its direct consequences for Christianity and Christian self-understanding, would now have to be seen as occurring *after* not *before* 1 Clement, so that 1 Clement would be a witness to a much more primitive theological milieu than has previously been considered the case. Understanding that milieu via 1 Clement can, in turn, have significant consequences for interpreting New Testament works written after circa AD 70.

3.1.C First Clement's Relationship with the Apostles Peter and Paul

If 1 Clement were dated in circa AD 70, its relevance for understanding the importance of Peter and Paul in the early Church could be increased. With the date of AD 96, the letter was simply too far removed from the lifetimes of the Apostles to have anything but a commemorative value. On the other hand, if the letter was written very few years after their deaths, the veracity of 1 Clement's account would be enhanced. For example, 1 Clement 5:7 is the source for the belief that Paul had in fact reached Spain on one of his missionary journeys. First Clement is likewise an important witness for the tradition that both Peter and Paul were in fact martyred at Rome. More than for these details, however, an earlier 1 Clement would help us understand better what have been called the Petrine and Pauline 'trajectories.'[125] That is to say, the effects of the influence on the Church of the historical Peter and Paul naturally continue to the present day. It is the task of the church historian and theologian to trace the effects of this influence accurately, thereby illustrating and explaining part of what is meant by the dogmatic formula "apostolic" as applied by the Roman Catholic Church to herself. It is significant, as noted above, that 1 Clement apparently knows of only two "Apostles" by name and they are Peter and Paul. We have taken this fact as an additional sign of the letter's early date

125 J. Robinson and H. Koster, *Trajectories Through Early Christianity*, pp. 167 ff.

inasmuch as the Synoptic tradition, with which 1 Clement was not familiar and on which he does not depend, will prefer to speak of the "Twelve" which would eventually be practically equated with the Apostles. Thus the familiar phrase "the twelve Apostles." But what of 1 Clement and his primitive sounding "two Apostles"? It is possible that this twin influence of the Apostles Peter *and* Paul can do much to explain 1 Clement. It can explain, for example, the very occasion of the letter. If written in circa AD 70, so soon after their dominant personal influence was removed from the Church by their deaths, it can be reasonably hypothesized that it was the very death of Paul which was the condition for the possibility of the Corinthian revolt in the first place. After all, the Corinthian community, as reflected in Paul's two canonical letters to them, had shown early signs of a similar rebelliousness, to which even 1 Clement explicitly alludes. First Clement can therefore be a witness to the effects of the death of the Apostle, i.e. the outbreak of the revolt against the presbyters, some of whom he had even appointed.[126] This outbreak, in turn, can be linked, at least in part, to the "charismatic" nature of the Corinthian church. Thus Paul can increasingly be viewed, not so much as the promoter of charismatic church structure, but as its opponent insofar as it threatened the unity and peace of the local church. The fact that 1 Clement is addressed to a *Pauline* church, but with clear roots also in the Petrine mission, can likewise help us see how Paul's influence survives his physical death. In a sense, it was because 1 Clement saw the Roman community, so recently led by the now deceased Apostles Peter and Paul, as heir to the Petrine and Pauline mission that the audacious-interference in the affairs of the Corinthian church could have been contemplated in the first place. Paul lives on in 1 Clement, as it were, since this letter, like Paul's own, is addressed to the Corinthian church and is explicitly corrective, as Paul himself had been often enough.

This continuation of the Pauline trajectory is not a figment of our imagination, either, since 1 Clement 47:1–4 appeals precisely to the canonical 1 Corinthians as a precedent for his present action. We might hypothesize then that the future interventions of the Roman church, insofar as 1 Clement contributes a precedent for them, are the result of a confluence of the Petrine *and* Pauline trajectories, a combination reflected traditionally in many other ways as well by what will later become the Roman Papacy.[127]

---

126 Cf. Y. Talmon, quoted in Gager, *op. cit.*, p. 28, in "Pursuit of the Millenium: The Relation between Religious and Social Change," *Archives Europeennes de Sociologie*, p. 137: "in many cases leaders functioned as a symbolic focus of identification rather than as sources of authority and initiative"; "... death, imprisonment or mysterious absence have increased their stature and enhanced their authority." Still it must be recognized that Paul's death had a *different* effect in Rome than it had in Corinth. In Rome, he was revered perhaps more in death than he was in life. In Corinth, the community submitted to him while he was alive, and when he died, the factious elements who opposed him became dominant. For the effect of a charismatic leader after death, cf. J. Gager, *Kingdom and Community*, 28.

127 For 1 Clement as the successor of Paul, cf. J. Fuellenbach, *op. cit.*, p. 22; L. Sanders, *L'Hellénisme*

3.1.D *The Episcopate and Presbyterate in an Earlier 1 Clement*

As was discussed above, 1 Clement represents a stage of ecclesiastical organization in which the terms referring to particular offices in the Church were not yet completely fixed. His use of ἐπίσκοπος and πρεσβύτερος to describe the same persons and the same office is similar to that of the New Testament itself. Since the presbyters to whom 1 Clement refer are plural, when he applies the term

---

de Saint Clément, pp. 143ff. Cf. also Eusebius, HE 3,21: "at this time Clement was still governing the Romans and he also occupied the third place in the list of the bishops in Rome after Paul and Peter (μετὰ Παῦλόν τε καὶ Πέτρον ἐπισκοπευσάντων βαθμόν)." For the notion of the Apostle as a local church leader, cf. 1 Peter 5:1: "as a fellow elder (συμπρεσβύτερος) and a witness to the sufferings of Christ ..." This reference retains its significance even if 1 Peter is considered pseudonymous because the ancient attribution of the epistle to Peter is a sign that the real author saw himself in the Petrine tradition which saw no problem in the Apostle exercising a local church role. *Pace*, R. *Brown*, *Antioch and Rome*, p. 164, no. 349, "Similarly anachronistic is the later thesis that Peter served as bishop of Rome (or sometimes Peter and Paul as bishops!). Curiously enough this is often ardently defended by people who think that thus they are honoring Peter, not recognizing that apostles might regard being designated as local bishops as a failure to appreciate their unique role. Historically, Peter was an apostle who died at Rome. If part of his apostolate was exercised in that church, this did not make him a local church supervisor. Philippians 1:1 shows that Paul distinguished himself from bishops." *But*, 1) Philippians 1:1 does not clearly refer to *bishops* when it says ἐπίσκοποι; 2) 1 Peter 5:1 does seem to venerate the tradition that Peter *also* took his place among those who had a local church function; 3) if the Apostles did so act, it is not clear that they would have therefore given up their wider apostolic roles. Cf. also, the inscriptions in the Catacombs of St. Sylvester: "*Paule et Petre petite pro victore*" in *Archeologia Cristiana* by Pasquale Testini, p. 415. I note in both of these last citations, the name of Paul is mentioned *before* Peter. In this connection, cf. R. Brown, *The Church the Apostles Left Behind*, p. 76: "By the end of the century, in a letter of the Roman Church to Corinth (1 Clement 5:2–5), Peter and Paul have become church pillars. That very ordering or sequence of names, with Peter first, is consistent in the early Rome-related documents of church history; it indicates that the Pauline heritage is now filtered through the prism of Petrine Christianity."

Cf. also St. John Chrysostom, Περὶ Ἱεροσύνης 1, no. 88ff. Also, 32nd Homily on the Epistle to the Romans: "It is for this reason that I love Rome, though I might praise it for other reasons ... but passing over all these, I call it blessed because Paul while he wrote to them, and so loved them that he preached to them and ended his life among them. ... Like a great and strong body it has two shining eyes, namely the bodies of those two saints. ... Hence Paul shall be rapt up, hence also Peter. Consider with awe what a spectacle Rome shall behold: Paul rising suddenly from that shrine along with Peter." I note again the priority given to Paul. There can hardly be anything more obvious in Christian artistic tradition, especially at Rome, than that the Apostles Peter and Paul are almost always depicted together, not exactly as a couple, but as two panels of the same dyptich. No clearer examples need be found than the twin statues of Peter and Paul at St. Peter's Basilica, and the twin statues again at St. Paul's. There is a rare explicit allusion to the Papacy's succession from Peter and Paul in a radio message given by John XXIII shortly before the opening of the Vatican Council II. First he quoted Innocent III, who recalled the two founders of earthly Rome, Romulus and Remus. Then he recalled the memory of Peter and Paul: "*duo fratres secundum fidem, Petrus et Paulus, qui urbem istam spiritualiter fundaverunt* ..." (Innocentii III, Sermo XXII). John XXIII went on to say: "In forma piu mite, l'umile *successors di Pietro e di Paolo* nel governo e nell'apostolato della Chiesa Cattolica, in questa vigil ia della riunione conciliare, ama rivolgersi ..." (*Discorsi, Messaggi, Colloqui del S. Padre Giovanni XXIII*, vol.IV, p. 527) (emphasis mine).

ἐπίσκοπος to these same people, it is clear that the term cannot be translated "bishop", as some modern translations of similar New Testament texts do.[128] This insight is, of course, hardly new but 1 Clement would give important confirmation to the scholarly insistence that "bishop," despite its etymological affinity to ἐπί σκοπος, is not the correct translation of that term as used in circa AD 70.[129]

The question naturally arises whether the monepiscopate existed at all in circa AD 70. It can be said that 1 Clement provides no proof that it did. This thesis has asserted that the Apostle Paul would have exercised what is later understood to be the episcopal role: individual personal oversight of the local church. He does this as a function of his apostleship, not as a *monepiskopos,* strictly so-called. Nor does this imply that he had necessarily to reside at Corinth while he exercised the role of principal overseer for the Christian community there. He did that rather by visiting that local church from time to time and by writing letters to the faithful there. It does, however, imply that while Paul lived, unless he himself relinquished or delegated this individual responsibility for oversight to someone else, he himself was able to exercise it without prejudice to his apostolic role. The rivalry within the Corinthian church, recalled by 1 Clement by citing the factionalism surrounding Cephas, Paul, and Apollos, may even have been an early impulse toward the selection of individual leaders or "bishops" in the later sense of the term. But with its circa AD 70 date, 1 Clement may well reflect a period in which a monepiscopal *successor* to the Apostles had not yet emerged, either at Rome or at Corinth.

It would be difficult to explain why, if there had been a *monepiskopos* at Rome at the time, 1 Clement would make no mention of him, nor allude to his authority. The same is true of the situation in Corinth: it seems quite unlikely that a monepiscopal government existed at Corinth since 1 Clement never mentions such a person, nor indicates that he too had been ousted with the presbyters, nor appeals to him for his help in setting the situation there right again. It is true that there *may* have been an individual who, like Timothy and Titus in the New Testament, personally exercised the role of overseer in Rome, but it is strange that 1 Clement never alludes to such a thing. On the other hand, there is no need to insist that monepiscopacy succeed to the apostolic government immediately, with no interval. In this sense we can see that there was most probably no apostolic appointment of a monepiscopal successor.

128 Cf. 1 Timothy 3:1 in the *RSV*: "If any one aspires to the office of bishop he desires a noble task."

129 Cf. *supra*, no. 99. More recently, however, some scholars have begun to prefer the construct term "presbyter-bishop" to denote those who held *episkopē*, but who are not single-bishops, and are sometimes called *presbyteroi*. Unwieldiness apart, the term is a) not used historically as such; b) *episkopē* or "oversight" does not exclude its being shared, even in modern bishop-priest-deacon structures; and c) always runs the risk of retrojecting later prerogatives of *bishops* (ordination for example) back into the period when the ecclesial structure was presbyteral, without demonstrable justification. I think it is sufficient to note the terminological confusion of the period without minting a *tertium quid* term to denote someone who is less than a bishop, cf. E. Jay, "From Presbyter-Bishops to Bishops and Presbyters."

Since 1 Clement clearly makes the point that the apostolic appointment of *presbyters* prevents their subsequent removal by the community, it is unthinkable that, had the Apostles also designated their monepiscopal successors, 1 Clement would have made no mention of that fact. It would have greatly reinforced his argument that his orders (that the Corinthian presbyters be restored) likewise enjoyed apostolic authority and should be obeyed. But it is striking that the argument from personal authority is not made in 1 Clement.

But while 1 Clement shows no knowledge of *monepiscopoi*, his witness to the tradition of the presbyter or elder is quite solid, and made the more so because of a probable circa AD 70 date. When 1 Clement had been thought to have been written in circa AD 96, the references he made to presbyters being appointed by the Apostles themselves were more easily dismissed as simplistic reconstructions of a now distant past with which the author was not himself personally familiar.[130] In the present case, with the letter written so soon after the deaths of the Apostles in his own community, 1 Clement can be seen to be a witness of the apostolic practice itself.

The fact that he asserts that presbyters were appointed by the Apostles cannot be ignored, and he therefore provides confirmation of the Catholic interpretation of the handing on of Holy Orders. Still, he is not a witness to the laying on of hands,[131] and when 1 Clement speaks of an Apostolic "Succession" he is referring, not to individual bishops replacing the Apostles, but of *presbyters* doing so. For 1 Clement, it is the presbyters who "succeed" to the Apostles in their role of governing the local church. The implications of this for Catholic theology shall have to be considered at greater length elsewhere, but 1 Clement will not allow what is said of elders to be confused with what may eventually be claimed for bishops.[132]

Here, it may be well to note that 1 Clement's insistence on the fact that at least some of the ousted presbyters had been appointed by the Apostles themselves or later on "by other eminent men" is an important indication not only that the Apostles appointed presbyters, but that 1 Clement admits of no other mechanism by which one became a presbyter than by appointment. This will in turn be significant as one approaches a study of the monarchical bishop in subsequent church history. More specifically, it is of key importance to see that not even the later episcopal lists, which speak solely of individual bishops, ever imply that one bishop appointed his successor *as a bishop*. He may very well, however, have appointed him *as a presbyter*. First Clement seems, then, to provide support for the later theory of Apostolic Succession of bishops coming *through* the continuous series of *presbyteral appointments*, or as later language will choose to say, ordinations. In this

130 Cf. R. Brown, *Antioch and Rome*, 174: "If one must conclude from this clear evidence that 1 Clement paints an over-simplified picture of the apostles' appointment of presbyter-bishops ..."

131 Cf. R. Brown, *Priest and Bishop*, 84.

132 Cf. *supra*, nos. 14 and 100.

sense 1 Clement will be at least implicitly compatible with the subsequent claim that, while bishops may not have chosen their successors, it was their exclusive right to appoint presbyters.

3.1.E *The Implications for Determining 1 Clement's Position on Roman Primacy and Papacy*

At the very outset of this paper it was pointed out that 1 Clement is actually an anonymous letter. It is written, it says, by "The Church of God which sojourns at Rome." We have drawn several conclusions from the fact that the letter does not reflect monepiscopacy, among which is the key point that Eusebius, who had provided us with the circa AD 96 date for 1 Clement in the first place, is irrelevant to a determination of the date of the letter since, when he spoke of Clement, he was clearly speaking of a *monepiskopos*. With the assertion, then, that 1 Clement is not a monepiscopal letter, comes the necessary conclusion that it cannot be a papal letter either for the simple reason that the Pope, as the individual personal leader of the Roman Church, is therefore also its *monepiskopos*. If we can successfully argue to a circa AD 70 for 1 Clement by demonstrating that the author of 1 Clement is not writing as a *monepiskopos*, that earlier date will also require us to recognize that 1 Clement is of little use as a proof of an early papal intervention, as was so often the thesis of older Catholic apologists.

One can however make a distinction between primacy and papacy. Primacy refers principally to the notion that the Roman Church *as church* exercised some kind of superior oversight over other churches. Papacy means that the bishop of Rome is also the person in whom the principal authority rests for the government of the universal church. This distinction makes it possible to admit, on one hand, that papacy is hardly present in 1 Clement because its author is not asserting any personal authority. On the other hand, 1 Clement should be considered for the extraordinary and unique thing it is: the intervention of the Roman Church in the internal affairs of another church. As was suggested above, the fact that the two Apostles, Peter and Paul, exercised their authority and died at Rome, and for all practical purposes were the *two* Apostles known to the Church of Rome, constituted a kind of precedent. Both Peter and Paul were associated not only with Rome but with large areas of the Gentile mission. First Clement, in its correction of the Corinthian community, necessarily has to fall within the Pauline tradition exemplified by the New Testament's 1 and 2 Corinthians, as we said above. As such, then, it would represent, not the fully developed papacy, but a *phase of the process which would later result in papacy*. This early phase is nevertheless marked by an incipient assertion of Roman *primacy* and its early circa AD 70, date makes such an assertion the more significant.[133]

133 Even Harnack would agree that 1 Clement represents a "first step" in what would later develop more fully into Roman Primacy. Cf. J. Fuellenbach, *op. cit.*, p. 31 *et passim*.

The larger doctrinal question here, is not whether there is to be found in 1 Clement some sign of intermediate steps toward papacy, or whether 1 Clement supports the notion of ecclesiastical office, but whether or not, for the Church at large, an argument can be made for the *normativity* of such tenets for the Church today.

We will turn now in a second section to consider this and other more general implications of an earlier 1 Clement for Roman Catholic theology.

3.2 Implications for Catholic Theology in General

3.2.A A Theology of Ecclesiastical Office

In 1976, Bernard Cooke wrote, regarding the precise meaning and origin of the terms *ἀπόστολος, ἐπίσκοπος,* and *πρεσβύτερος*:

> The scholarly writings of the past two decades ... appear to have thoroughly sifted, analyzed and commented upon whatever data is available to us. Congar, von Campenhausen, Schweizer, Daniélou, Colson, Kung and Schnackenburg, to name only some of the more prominent authors, have dealt with the matter in detail and from various perspectives. To quite an extent a consensus emerges concerning the general picture, but disagreement on details (some of them fairly important) seems unresolvable, unless some new data is discovered (which seems unlikely) or some fresh approach to understanding the historical evidence appears.[134]

While a mere dating hypothesis of a single letter can hardly be thought to revolutionize the whole of Catholic theology, it is plausible that the early date for 1 Clement might provide some "new evidence" for the on-going examination of the historical and theological foundations of a contemporary understanding of Christian ministry and Church office.

The underlying question, again, is not whether the Apostles appointed presbyters but whether that apostolic practice can be construed as somehow *normative* for the Church for all ages. Naturally, such a question could easily be the subject of an entire thesis itself, and cannot therefore be settled here. Still, some observations can be made which may prove useful in the overall discussion, with particular reference to 1 Clement.

There is no question *that 1 Clement himself* believes that the presbyterate as he knew it *is* to be considered normative. This is particularly important since he does so in the face of an explicit call for an alternative to the presbyteral structure that had been in place at Corinth before the presbyters were dismissed. This shows

134 B. Cooke, *Ministry to Word and Sacraments*, p. 53, no. 46.

that 1 Clement is not unaware, i.e. not simplistic or naive, about the fact that there were indeed, "pluralistic" approaches to church order, but in comparison with the presbyterate which is of apostolic origin, he judges these alternatives illegitimate.

There is likewise no question that the Catholic Church has followed this same approach and considers the presbyterate normative.

Moreover, it is historically demonstrable that from the Fourth to the Sixteenth century no one in either the Eastern or Western Churches would seriously challenge the normativity of the presbyterate.

On the negative side, however, the following points should be kept in mind.

First of all, 1 Clement is not part of the canon of Sacred Scripture. While it did win some local acceptance as a work of the New Testament, and was thus included in the codices Alexandrinus and Constantinopolitanus, it was never universally recognized as enjoying the particular authority reserved for the Bible alone. Thus, the fact that a particular tenet appears as part of the doctrine of 1 Clement does not in and of itself require that the Christian Church accept that tenet as binding.

Secondly, there is much in 1 Clement which even advocates of a strong Roman Papacy would not accept. His attitude toward the presbyteral college appears to leave little room for episcopal government as it is known today in the Catholic and Orthodox Churches.

Thirdly, the idea that a Church, as Church, and not the bishop of that Church, should write a letter of correction to another Church, can hardly be considered normative for Catholic ecclesiology.[135]

Fourthly, we cannot retroject on to 1 Clement the whole complex of contemporary questions which are generated by our present ecclesial situation in which Christianity is divided, not only between East and West (which nevertheless still agree on the normativity of the presbyterate) but also in literally hundreds of loosely connected or even wholly autonomous bodies which identify themselves as Christian but which may never have had a presbyteral structure at all. First Clement was reacting to a community that had had a presbyteral structure which it then rejected.

To summarize: a revised date for 1 Clement will surely affect not only how the letter itself should be interpreted but also how that letter has in turn been used in the broader field of theological inquiry. The exact consequences shall have to be studied further in each individual case, but 1 Clement's early witness not only to the existence of the presbyterate, but to its *normativity* cannot be ignored in any objective historicotheological study of the origins of Christian church order in the period immediately after the Apostles themselves.

135 Cf. example of Roman presbyterate which wrote to Cyprian: G. D'Ercole, "The Presbyteral Colleges in the Early Church," *Concilium*, vol. 17, pp. 28–29.

3.2.B Pluralism in the Early Church

We have seen that 1 Clement itself is a strong statement for the normativity of the presbyteral college form of Church government. The restoration of the Corinthian presbyters is the single greatest purpose of the letter. It is true that there are several indications that such presbyteral government was not universal. The Didache for example advises its recipients to "appoint ἐπισκόπους ... for yourselves."[136] But such spontaneous appointment of leaders is hardly 1 Clement's notion of proper Church government. It may even be that that is exactly what the Corinthians did which precipitated the ouster of their elders. We do not know. The letters of Ignatius, famous as they are for their insistence on the tri-partite hierarchy of bishop, presbyters, and deaconate, are nevertheless also a sign that he felt the need to promote this format precisely because it was *not* shared by some of the communities to which he wrote, or, if it was the prevailing form of government, it was by no means universally accepted. In any case, there can be no question that there were widely divergent views in the early Church regarding how the community should be organized.

First Clement is related to this controversy in several important ways.

First, the letter itself, while often cited as a clear instance of the Roman ecclesiology, is nonetheless also a further indication that pluralist notions of church order were common in the first Christian communities. He would have already known of Paul's struggles to maintain the unity of the Corinthian church in his 1 and 2 Corinthians. First Clement is in direct continuity with Paul's interventions. Therefore, 1 Clement gives us both an insight into the dissension which immediately followed Paul's death *and* an early effort (successful, as it turned out) to make presbyteral structure the norm in the local churches.

Secondly, besides being a proof of pluralist ecclesiologies, 1 Clement points to the presbyteral structure as a means of safeguarding the integrity of the community's faith. Unfortunately, he does not go into detail about the reasons why the presbyters were removed. He says, broadly speaking, that their ouster was caused by jealousy and strife. Such moralizing regarding the true motives for their ouster may be due to the fact that 1 Clement does not know what exact doctrines the new leaders of the Corinthian Church espouse. Or, perhaps, he does not want to enter into an ideological or theological debate with them and strategically confines his argument to the necessity of bringing back the presbyters. But we should look beyond the merely structural side of the question to determine the deeper theological issues underlying the ouster in the first place. Were the revolutionaries Gnostics? Did they propound a "new gospel" because of which they were necessarily at odds with the presbyters appointed by Paul? These questions, while interesting, are notoriously difficult, and probably impossible to answer with certainty. This is because the revolutionaries did not probably all belong to any one ideological

136 Didache, 15:1.

side. In fact, the charismatic nature of the Corinthian community that Paul knew would lead us rather to believe that they were most *disunited* in their Christian beliefs. What is important here is not the need for presbyters, for presbyters' sake, but the need to return to a more fundamental issue, namely why were the original presbyters appointed in the first place? Not, certainly, just to fulfill some abstract need to have a presbyteral collegiate church order. First Clement shows us instead that the ouster of the presbyterate is linked to a host of other disunifying elements within the community, which he describes in terms of hatred, anger, jealousy, and so on. First Clement's choice for a particular form of church order, the presbyterate, is not simply an answer to the question of *how* to organize the Church, but *why do so*. His famous answer of apostolic succession, as later generations of theological discussion will show, is not merely to determine which are the legitimate leaders of the community, but first and foremost to provide a guarantee that the communities' beliefs, articulated by the leaders, are in conformity with the apostolic doctrine. It is the doctrine and not the polity for polity's sake which is the key element.[137]

The classical formulation of the question of pluralism, then, may be mistaken in itself. It tended to see the presbyteral order as over and against the charismatic order. The choice for the presbyterate, though, is not so much a choice of structure as it is a choice for fidelity to the apostolic teaching, to which the apostolic appointees are the witnesses. Apostolic succession then is principally concerned with the correctness of the doctrine of the Church and represents a choice for the doctrine of the Apostles, as transmitted by the presbyters whom they appointed. This presbyteral structure, with its apostolic origin, is therefore not *per se* opposed to charisms, just as the apostolic structure, personified by Paul, was not *per se* opposed to charismatic activity. This is because it was the fundamental conviction of Paul and the charismatic Corinthian believers that *his* authority and *their* gifts both had God as their origin and cause. It would be a wild generalization and a calumny to claim that persons gifted by the charisms of Christian faith somehow automatically opposed the Apostle. If Paul would have to criticize the Corinthians for some of their behavior, it was never to criticize them for their χαρίσματα which, he acknowledged, came from God.[138]

In criticism of 1 Clement, it may be concluded that his heavy accent on moral defects in the revolutionaries can obscure what is a more basic issue in the entire struggle over the presbyters, namely the underlying doctrinal dissent to which 1 Clement hardly alludes. Further, his extended argument for order within the community does insufficient justice to the need to determine what is the basic

137 J. Ratzinger, "Primacy, Episcopate and Apostolic Succession", in *Quaestiones Disputatae* 4, p. 46–47: "'Tradition' is never a simple, anonymous passing on of doctrine, but is personal, is the living word, concretely realized in the faith. And 'succession' is not a taking over of official powers, which are at the disposal of their possessor, but is rather a dedication to the word, an office of bearing witness to the treasure with which one has been entrusted."

138 1 Corinthians 7:7; 12:27ff.

source for unity within the Christian Church. That source is not principally the hierarchy, but the Risen Lord. The hierarchy serves that unity, it does not create it. First Clement by so emphasizing the importance of the presbyterate, for the sake of his immediate goal of having the Corinthian elders restored, risks distorting for us the real value of the presbyterate. By failing to identify more accurately the causes of the Corinthian revolt, 1 Clement's solution can in turn generate distorted theological discussion which can lose sight of the more basic questions of faith which were at issue.

To put it more positively, 1 Clement, especially if dated as early as ca AD 70, is a sign that Church structure is not incompatible with charisms *per se*, as long as those charisms are not exercised at the expense of Church unity. First Clement's doctrine is that the presbyterate comes from the Apostles themselves and that, therefore, in accepting the elders back, the Corinthian Church will not be giving up their identity as a charismatic community precisely because those charisms likewise coexisted with presbyteral structure during the Apostles' own lifetime. Rather, in welcoming back the presbyters as persons whose comprehension of and fidelity to the gospel were recognized by the Apostles themselves, the Corinthians would be assuring their own continuity with the Apostles and thus with the doctrine whose guarantors were the Apostles, and they alone.

3.2.C *Christian Eschatology*

This question is enormously complex, and we cannot pretend to be able to resolve it here. As was noted above, and in a parallel line with what has just been said about pluralism, 1 Clement provides us with the insight that the presbyterate, or any structured form of church order for that matter, is not of itself incompatible with eschatological belief. We have already pointed out that 1 Clement, too, shows his own belief in the future return of the Lord. It has been intimated that the specific belief that the Lord's return would occur *soon* may not be a sign of protochristianity, but a sign of a re-judaizing tendency, i.e. a *later* development.[139] Whatever the case, 1 Clement with its eschatological beliefs side by side with an insistence on the presbyteral form of Church government is a proof that Church structure can co-exist with eschatological hope.

3.2.D *Implications of an Earlier 1 Clement for Understanding Ignatius of Antioch*

Ignatius of Antioch will necessarily command significant attention in early Patristic studies simply because so much and such varied material of his is still extant. It was noted above that Ignatius' conviction that without a bishop "the name of church is not even given," strikes us as a decidedly more developed state of ecclesiological practice than could be deduced from a letter like 1 Clement. It was Robinson who argued that, if 1 Clement were to be dated in circa AD 96, not all

139 Cf. *supra*, no. 104.

that much time would appear to have elapsed before Ignatius' day, which scholarly consensus would locate in the period between AD 107 and 110.[140] This was an auxiliary argument for agreeing that the time of 1 Clement is substantially earlier in order to allow for the intervening development to take place which culminated in Ignatius' episcopal doctrine.

An earlier 1 Clement, would help locate Ignatius on a more linear track of development from the simple presbyteral doctrine of 1 Clement. In effect, then, 1 Clement should not be seen to conflict with Ignatius' monepiscopal emphasis since 1 Clement does not represent Roman church order shortly before Ignatius, i.e. in AD 96, but *substantially* before, i.e. in AD 70. Thus, 1 Clement can be seen to provide a precious and primitive defense of the apostolic origin of church order in itself, while Ignatius gives us the earliest extant specification of that order in its tripartite form.

Further, to accept an earlier 1 Clement is to agree that his theology, originating in Rome, is not all that highly developed. By contrast, it is Ignatius' *non*-Roman ecclesiology which is remarkably more detailed. This is only to say that, with an earlier 1 Clement, perhaps more particular attention can be paid to Ignatius when he is appreciated in his own right and not seen as a mere mouthpiece for a provincial Roman theology,[141] or, worse, an isolated innovator.

3.2.E Implications of an Early Date of 1 Clement for Early Church Historiography, e.g. Eusebius of Caesarea

It will be recalled that Eusebius gives us two pieces of information which have had enormous influence on the interpretation of 1 Clement. One, from *Historia Ecclesiastica* 3,13–15, is our source for connecting Clement and his episcopate with the year AD 96. Because Eusebius linked the well known dates of the Roman Emperors' reigns with the series of Roman ἐπίσκοποι, it was taken for granted that Clement began his episcopate in circa AD 95, that is the year before Domitian's death in AD 96. The second piece of information we get from Eusebius is that from HE 5,6,1-2, when he records that it was in the time of this Clement that a serious revolt broke out among the Corinthians, and Clement wrote to them and succeeded in resolving the dispute. This is certainly a reference to the central point of 1 Clement. It seemed therefore to follow that 1 Clement was written shortly before the death of Domitian, i.e. in AD 96. As we saw above, modern historiographers are much more critical of Eusebius than they were in the past.[142] They point out that his list of Roman ἐπίσκοποι came from Irenaeus, and that he was clearly not an eye-witness to the events he described. Furthermore, Eusebius was motivated to

140 Cf. *supra*, no. 116.

141 Cf. J. F. McCue, "The Roman Primacy in the Patristic Era: 1. The Beginnings through Nicea," *Papal Primacy and the Universal Church*, eds. P. C. Empie and T. A. Murphy, p. 45.

142 Cf. *supra*, no.15.

write the *Historia Ecclesiastica* in part to show the legitimacy of the episcopal form of government of his day by relating it in an unbroken series or succession with the *ἐπίσκοποι* who had preceded his contemporaries, going back to the Apostles themselves. In any case, the earlier the period, the less reliable Eusebius can be shown to be. As far as the Roman succession immediately after Peter is concerned, his reliability is greatly conditioned by the lack of firm archeological or documentary evidence. Here is where the new date of 1 Clement may be important. If it can be shown that this document was not written while its author was a *monepiskopos*, the second of Eusebius' two points can be shown to be misleading. It is possible that Eusebius had information that the letter now known as 1 Clement was indeed written by the same Clement who later became *ἐπίσκοπος* at Rome. After all, the manuscript attribution of the letter to Clement is unanimous, and there is no serious reason to doubt its accuracy. On the other hand, since the letter shows no trace of monepiscopacy, one would have to distinguish within the career of Clement between the time when he was a prominent member of the Roman Christian community and the time when he was its *ἐπίσκοπος*. For this discrepancy, which appears to have been unrecognized or perhaps even "homogenized" by Eusebius, 1 Clement nevertheless provides important evidence, and allows us to approach Eusebius more critically. He was, after all, utterly reliant on his sources, whatever they were. His error here, in not recognizing that the same Clement could have been *both* author of 1 Clement *and ἐπίσκοπος* at Rome, but at *different* times, seems an innocent enough mistake. For making it, though, and for not realizing that 1 Clement could have been written as early as AD 70, Eusebius can no longer be seen as ruling our interpretation of 1 Clement, but vice-versa. First Clement provides us here with new evidence to re-read Eusebius, not rejecting out of hand the information he provides, but not at the same time giving it *a priori* acceptance.

3.3 Conclusion

Perhaps more than any other document, 1 Clement's meaning has been closely linked with its proposed date. When that date was fixed as circa AD 96, the letter was taken to reflect the state of theology and ecclesiastical order in Rome and Corinth toward the end of the first century. If, as this thesis has argued at length, its date is rather circa AD 70, the time is set back over twenty-five years, and consequently, the meaning of 1 Clement shall have to be revised accordingly.

Its significance for Catholic theology will likely be enhanced by an earlier dating hypothesis since its witness to the foundation of the presbyterate in the apostolic period can now be seen as the testimony, not of a far removed recipient of a tradition, but of an eye witness, for the Apostles would now be of 1 Clement's own generation, a claim he himself makes.[143] On the other hand, 1 Clement dated in circa AD 70 will challenge Catholic theology to be attentive to the pluralistic

143 1 Clement 5:1.

situation of the formative period of the Church and to have a more nuanced appreciation of the complex of causes which need to be identified in an historically accurate analysis of the origins of church order.

Appendix
External Evidence for an "Early" Clement

The question might well be raised whether there exist any indications, independent of the New Testament or the text of 1 Clement, which would support the conclusion of this thesis that 1 Clement dates from a period much earlier than is commonly presumed, perhaps as early as AD 70. The answer is that there are indeed. A number of references to Clement, the probable author, by early Christian writers can be listed which may help to view the AD 70 dating hypothesis in a more sympathetic light.

We have already seen that the traditional date of circa AD 96 for 1 Clement comes from Eusebius who, in his *Historia Ecclesiastica* (circa AD 310–325), provided a list of Roman bishops which for the first time was coordinated with the well known regnal years of the Roman Emperors, thus effectively giving the years when these bishops were believed to have held episcopal office in Rome. This was not the first of such episcopal lists, and Eusebius no doubt made use of two previous lists, one by Hegissipus and the other by Irenaeus. Hegissipus (circa AD 170) comes down to us only through *Historia Ecclesiastica* iv, 22, but he does not himself mention Clement. Irenaeus (circa AD 180) is extant in the Latin *Adversus Haereses*, and in a much shorter Greek text. He gives us the earliest Roman episcopal list in which Clement is named, and in the third place after the Apostles, after Linus and Anencletus. This is the order followed by Eusebius and is the one accepted by almost everyone today.[144]

Shortly after Eusebius, however, in AD 354, an unknown compiler prepared a list of Roman bishops which differs significantly from Eusebius's. This list, usually called the "Liberian Catalogue" since Liberius is the last mentioned Roman bishop and it may have been he who had the list drawn up, places Clement immediately after Peter and Linus:

> Clemens ann ix m xi dies xii fuit temporibus Galbae et Vespasiani
> a cons Traculi et Italici usque Vespasiano vi et Tito.

Lightfoot calculated that the consulship of Traculus and Italicus was in AD 68 and that the sixth year of Vespasian and Titus should mean AD 76.[145]

The Catalogue forms just one section of a far larger work which includes, among other things, a list of the consuls of Rome from the beginning to AD 354 (whence the original manuscript's probable date) and a chronicle of the city of Rome until the death of Licinius in AD 324.[146] From the title leaf it is clear that it is the

---

144 Cf. *L'Annuario Pontificio*, 1988, p. 7–8; J. N. D. Helly, *The Oxford Dictionary of Popes*, pp. 5–8.

145 Lightfoot, *op. cit.*, p. 253.

146 H. Stem, *Le Calendrier* de 354: *Etude sur son texte et ses illustrations*, p. 113.

work of the famous calligrapher, Furius Dionysius Filocalus, whose name will later be connected with the renowned epigrams of Pope Damasus (AD 366–384).[147] In any case, the work is of the highest quality and was most likely composed as some kind of a present for a certain Valentinus, whose identity remains dubious.[148]

Lightfoot, in an exhausting if not exhaustive analysis, makes use of the previous studies made of the manuscript by Mommsen, Lipsius, and Duchesne.[149] He takes great pains to show that the episcopal list is far from perfect. First there are the manuscript problems; then there are the multiple probable sources on which the Catalogue was originally based; next there are the chronological inaccuracies within the list itself, as compared with the Consular Fasti of the same manuscript. Finally, there are the numerous problems and discrepancies with the later bishops, especially from Pontianus (circa AD 231–235) onward.[150] Very little of this need concern us here, however, since it does not have to do with Clement.

What is important in an evaluation of Lightfoot's study is his assertion that, "the date of Clement's Epistle is fixed with a fair degree of certainty at AD 95 or 96, as it was written during or immediately after the persecution of Domitian. This year therefore must fall within the episcopate of Clement."[151] Here we have Lightfoot proposing, as a test of the historical reliability of the Liberian Catalogue, the date of 1 Clement. In other words, since the Liberian Catalogue places Clement's episcopacy in the years circa AD 68–76, it must not be trustworthy since it is fairly certain that 1 Clement was written in the 90's. As we have seen all along, *this is precisely what needs to be proven, not presumed.* We have also seen that even Lightfoot was quite cautious about describing the author of 1 Clement as a monarchical bishop, but here he seems to presume that the letter had to have been written during his "episcopate".[152]

Despite Lightfoot's predictable negative conclusions, the following points seem nevertheless worth reviewing.

1. The Liberian Catalogue *postdates* Eusebius. Therefore, it is taking specific and pointed exception to the tradition represented by Irenaeus and Eusebius that Clement succeeded Anencletus.
2. Likewise, the Liberian Catalogue completely disagrees with Eusebius's coordination of Clement's episcopate with the reign

147 Ibid., 46.

148 Ibid., 357–358: "C'est un ouvrage de luxe créé et exécuté pour une occasion précise par un artiste de grand mérite. Sans doute, d'autres calendriers illustrés en forme de *codex* ont-ils été en usage à Rome à cette époque. Celui de Filocalus n'en est pas moins une oeuvre d'art d'un caractère tout à fait individuel."

149 Cf. T. Mommsen, *Auctores Antiquissimi*, vol. ix, pp. 13–38; R. A. Lipsius, *Die Papstverzeichnisse des Eusebios and der von ihm abhangigen Chronisten*; L. Duchesne, *Liber Pontificalis*, t. I.

150 Lightfoot, *op. cit.*, pp. 246–303.

151 Ibid., 342.

152 Cf. *supra*, no. 20.

of Domitian, placing it instead in the reign of Vespasian in the 70's.[153]

3. The list cannot be considered amateurish or a document of no consequence. One of the greatest calligraphers of the age wrote the original manuscript, and it was intended to be a work of the highest quality available.
4. The list, as the entire manuscript, is of certain *Roman* provenance, in contrast with both Irenaeus and Eusebius.
5. Because it contains such specific dating references (numbers of years, months, and days of office) it almost certainly derives from *documents* of the Roman Church archives.[154]

My conclusion is this: given the various manuscript problems and individual chronological discrepancies as traced by Lightfoot, the Liberian Catalogue *as a whole* cannot be accepted as a proof of one position or another regarding the date of 1 Clement. It does, however, express an important recollection of the Roman community which should not lightly be set aside. This recollection is all the more worthy of attention because it comes from Rome itself, and in all probability from some documentary source. Its importance is enhanced insofar as it is in open *dis*agreement with other known Roman episcopal lists. This discordance is even more interesting when it is noted what the list does *not* say: it makes no mention of 1 Clement. Its date, therefore, of the episcopate of Clement is not based on some theory about when 1 Clement was written. The Liberian Catalogue, while it may have been subsequently discounted for not being in agreement with the dominant Eusebian chronology, represents the *Roman* chronology and thus can make a serious claim to historical reliability at least insofar as it would record the memory of Clement as a leading figure in the Roman Church in the 70's. What the nature of his "leadership" or "episcopate" may have been is, for the present discussion, a separate question.

And the evidence for an "early" Clement continues. It has already been seen that Irenaeus placed Clement after both Linus and Anencletus, and that this was the order accepted by Eusebius. Irenaeus, however, did not make Eusebius's close coordinations with the regnal years of the Emperors, so that for him the exact dates of the episcopates of these early figures remained somewhat open. In the exact place where he places Clement in the third place (τρίτῳ τόπῳ) after the Apostles, Irenaeus also records that Clement's association with the Apostles was an intimate one:

153 We cannot be certain that the Compiler knew Irenaeus and/or Eusebius as such. But surely the claim must have been known at Rome that Clement succeeded Anencletus. If not, how is one to evaluate the fact that such an order was not known, even in Rome? We can conclude, then, that the Compiler was disagreeing with the Eusebian *order*.

154 Stern, *op. cit.*, p. 114.

> ... *μετὰ τοῦτον δὲ τρίτῳ τόπῳ ἀπὸ τῶν ἀποστόλων τὴν ἐπισκοπὴν κληροῦται Κλήμης, ὁ καὶ ἑορακὼς τοὺς μακαρίους ἀποστόλους καὶ συμβεβληκὼς αὐτοῖς, καὶ ἔτι ἔναυλον τὸ κήρυγμα τῶν ἀποστόλων καὶ τὴν παράδοσιν πρὸ ὀφθαλμῶν ἔχων, οὐ μόνος.*[155]

Tertullian (circa AD 200, and therefore considerably before Eusebius), says:

> Hoc enim modo ecclesiae apostolicae census suos deferunt sicut ... Romanorum (ecclesia) Clementem a Petro ordinatum (refert).[156]

Naturally Tertullian is using a technical language of his own day (*ordinatum*) but this does not detract from the tradition he represents that Clement had a close personal contact with Peter himself. Tertullian, then, would be a witness not only that Peter was of the same generation as Clement, but also that their association with each other occurred when Clement was already an adult.

Origen (AD 253) recalls Clement as *"apostolorum discipulus."*[157] Optatus (circa AD 370) writes,

> Ergo cathedram unicam, quae est prima de dotibus sedit prior Petrus, Lino successit Clemens, Clementi Anencletus.[158]

One might speculate that Optatus depends here on material to which he was not himself a witness. On the other hand, *he* believed it to represent the correct view, and again, the very discordance between this information and the Eusebian order, in all probability already circulating as one opinion, is worthy of note. This exact citation does not help date 1 Clement with any greater certitude, but it does show that the "early" Clement hypothesis once enjoyed rather wide acceptance.

Important for this review of early Christian authors is the record provided by Jerome (circa AD 392). In one section of *De Viris Illustribus* he has this to say about the connection between Clement and the epistle to the Hebrews:

> Epistula quae fertur ad Hebraeos ... creditor ... vel ... vel ... vel Clementis Romanae postea ecclesiae episcopi, quem aiunt sententias Pauli proprio ordinasse et omasse sermone.[159]

155 IIE v, 6; *Adversus Haereses*, iii, 3,3.

156 *De Praescriptione Haereticorum*, 32.

157 *De Principiis*, ii, 3, 6.

158 *De Schismate Donati*, ii,3.

159 *De Viris Illustribus*, 5.

The similarity of style between Hebrews and 1 Clement has already been noticed above,[160] but this is an interesting external witness to a possible explanation of the causes. Further, Jerome gives us here an important perspective, often lost in the homogenizing tendency of Eusebius to locate all the events of an important ecclesiastical figure within the ambit of his later episcopate. Here, Jerome says that Hebrews was composed by Clement, who later became bishop. It is this perspective which may prove helpful in seeing how the same Clement may have written 1 Clement *before* taking charge of the Roman Church as its single bishop.

In a second section of the same work, Jerome writes:

> Clemens de quo apostolus Paulus ad Phillippenses scribens ait ... quartus post Petrum episcopus si quidem Linus fuit, tertius Anacletus, tametsi plerique Latinorum secundum apostolum Petrum putent fuisse Clementem.[161]

Again, we have Jerome witnessing to two *simultaneous* traditions within the Roman Church, namely that Clement succeeded Anencletus, third in line after Peter, or that he succeeded Peter directly. The fact that Jerome, while preferring the first, adds that the second is held by "*plerique Latinorum*" is fairly reliable evidence for the survival of a tradition for an "early" Clement among a considerable number of Romans. The additional point he makes, namely that Paul in Philippians 4:3 is referring to one and the same Clement who later became bishop of Rome,[162] is all the more interesting since Jerome does not seem to see any problem with this man, already an adult when he was Paul's companion, being more than fifty years older if he wrote 1 Clement in the middle 90's. But it needs to be seen that Jerome shows no sign of knowing 1 Clement was written that late. Therefore, while a witness of the "early" Clement tradition, because he records that many Romans of his day continued to think that Clement directly succeeded Peter as bishop of Rome, still Jerome is not quite a follower of the "late" Clement theory either, since he does not seem to know *when* Clement may have succeeded Anencletus, as he thinks was the case.

Finally, we can quote Augustine (circa AD 400) who was arguably at least as much in a position as anyone else to know the correct sequence:

> Petro enim successit Linus, Lino Clemens, Clementi Anencletus.[163]

160 Cf. *supra*, no. 86.

161 *De Viris Illustribus*, 15.

162 Cf. *supra*, no. 16.

163 Epist. LIII § 2.

What sense can be made of all this? It seems clear on one hand that the tradition for a "late" Clement, in Domitian's time, is a strong one, and in fact is the prevalent opinion even today. On the other hand, it can probably be maintained, without much fear of contradiction, that the very comprehensiveness of Eusebius's *Historia Ecclesiastica* and the fact that it is the exclusive source of information we have for many of the early events of church history effectively have assured that, in cases of doubt, historians tend to follow Eusebius. Still, we have seen that this is increasingly less the case today as more and more of Eusebius's discrepancies come to light.[164] At all events, one should avoid the view that the tradition of a "late" Clement is universal, as the above mentioned authors should show rather clearly. Very probably, the root cause of the confusion is whether or not 1 Clement 1:1 has anything to do with Domitian. As was seen above, whether that text has anything to do with persecution at all is a point open to great debate.[165] But, even if Domitian *had* a persecution, and even if one were to interpret 1 Clement 1:1 as signifying some type of anti-Christian harassment, there still is lacking any proof whatever that it is *Domitian's* persecution which is meant. We have seen that Eusebius certainly linked Clement to Domitian, and the majority have followed him. As this view prevailed, other witnesses to an "early" Clement were dismissed as misinformed. In effect, one has to ask whether there is any justification for continuing to link Clement to Domitian and thus to the AD 95–96 dating hypothesis. These further witnesses, completely independently of the text of 1 Clement, would seem to say there is not.

---

164 Cf. *supra*, no. 15.

165 Cf. *supra*, section 1.2.

Selected Bibliography

1. *Text*

Funk-Bihlmeyer-Schneelmelcher, Die apostolischen Väter. Vol.1, pp. 35–70. Tübingen, 1956.

Jaubert, Annie, *Clément de Rome: Epître aux Corinthiens*; Sources Chrétiennes. No. 167, pp. 98–204. Paris, 1971.

Lake, Kirsopp, *Apostolic Fathers I*; Loeb Classical Library. No. 24, pp. 8–120. London, 1977.

2. *Reference Works*

Vatican Council II: the Conciliar and Post Conciliar Documents, ed. Austin Flannery, OP. Dublin: 1980, 2nd ed.

A Patristic Greek Lexicon, ed. G. W. H. Lampe. Oxford: 1972.

Clavis Patrum Apostolicorum: Konkordanz zu den Schriften der apostolischen Väter. Ed. Henricus Kraft. München: 1963.

Enchiridion Symbolorum Definitionum et Declarationum de Rebus Fidei et Morum. Ed. Henricus Denzinger et Adolphus Schonmetzer, SJ. Freibourg: 1969, (33rd ed).

Concilium Tridentinum. Diariorum, Actorum, Epistularum, Tractuum Nova Collectio. Ed. Societas Goerresiana, XIII Vols. Freiburg, 1965–1985.

Biblia Patristica, *Index des citations et allusions bibliques dans la littérature Patristique*. Vol. I: Des Origines a Clément d'Alexandrie et Tertullien, 1975.

Blass, F. and Debrunner, A. *A Greek Grammar of the New Testament and Other Early Christian Literature*. Trans. Robert Funk. Chicago, 1962.

Corpus Inscriptionum Latinarum VI: Inscriptiones Urbis Romae Latinae. Pars 7. Indices Vocabulorum. Fasc. 11: D-F. Eds. Jory and Moore, 1975.

Oxford Classical Dictionary, 2nd ed. Eds. N. G. L. Hammond and H. H. Scullard. Oxford, 1970.

Schwyzeer, E. *Griechische Grammatik*, II. Munchen, 1950.

Bauer, W. and Griechische-Deutsch, *Wörterbuch zu den Schriften des Neuen Testaments und der übrigen urchristlichen Literatur.* Ste Auf. Berlin, 1958.

3. *Other Works Consulted*

Achtemcier, Paul J. "An Elusive Unity: Paul, Acts and the Early Church." *CBQ* 48 (1986): 1–26.

Ackroyd, P. R., and Evans, C. F., eds. *Cambridge History of the Bible.* Vol.I: *From the Beginnings to Jerome.* Cambridge, 1970.

Altaner, Berthold. *Patrology.* Trans. Hilda Graef. New York, 1961.

Appel, N. *Kanon und Kirche. Die Kanonkriese im heutigen Protestantismus als kontroverstheologisches Problem.* Paderborn, 1964.

Aquinas, S. Thomas. *Super Epistulas S. Pauli Lectura,* R. Co-ed. Vol. I. Epistulae ad Romanos, Corinthios et Galates. Paris, 1912.

Aubert, Roger, ed. *Historical Problems of Church Renewal,* "Concilium." Vol. 7. New York, 1965.

______. *Progress and Decline in the History of Church Renewal.* "Concilium." Vol. 27. New York, 1967.

Audet, J.-P., *La Didaché.* Etudes Bibliques. Paris, 1958.

Balthasar, Hans Urs von. "Gibt es ein »Römisches Prinzip«?" *Internationale Katholische Zeitschrift* 3 (1974): 285–288.

______. *The Office of Peter and the Structure of the Church.* Trans. Andre de Emery. San Francisco, 1986.

Bardy, G. "Expressions stoiciennes dans la Prima Clementis." *RSR* 12 (1922): 73–85.

______. "La Théologie de l'Eglise de Saint Clément de Rome à Saint Irénée." *Unam Sanctam* 13. Paris, 1945.

Barnard, L. W. "The Early Roman Church, Judaism and Jewish Christianity." *Anglican Theological Review* 49 (1967): 371–384.

______. "St. Clement of Rome and the Persecution of Domitian." *Studies in the Apostolic Fathers and Their Background.* Oxford, 1966. Pg. 518.

______. "Review of *Clemens Romanus und der Fruhkatholizismus* (by K. Beyschlag)." *Vigiliae Christianae* 23 (1969): 63–65.

Barrett, C. K. "The Apostles in and after the New Testament." *SEA* 21 (1956): 30–49.

______. *Church, Ministry and Sacraments in the New Testament Church.* Grand Rapids, 1985.

Bauer, Walter. *Orthodoxy and Heresy in Early Christianity.* Trans. Philadelphia Seminar on Christian Origins. Philadelphia, 1971.

______. *Handbuch zum Neuen Testament,* 3rd ed. Frankfurt, 1985.

______ and Paulsen, H. *Die Briefe des Ignatius von Antiochia und der Polykarperbrief.* Tubingen, 1985.

Bekes, Gerardo, J. "La successione nella tradizione apostolica: it problema fra la successione del ministero e la paradosis apostolica nel documento (BEM)." *Il*

Ministero Ordinato nel Dialogo Ecumenico: Scritti in onore di Gerardo J. Békés. Studia Anselmiana 92. Roma, 1985.

Bermejo, Luis M. *Towards Christian Reunion, Vatican II: Obstacles and Opportunities.* Anand (India), 1984.

Betz, O. "The Kerygma of Luke." *Interpretation* 22 (1968): 131–146.

Beyschlag, K. *Clemens Romanus und der Frühkatholizismus: Untersuchungen zu I Clemens* 1–7, BHTh 35. Tübingen, 1966.

Blank, Josef. *Vom Urchristentum zur Kirche.* Munchen, 1982.

Boismard, M. E. "Clément de Rome et l'Evangile de Jean." *RB* 55 (1948): 376–387.

Borgen, P. "From Paul to Luke: Observations Toward Clarification of the Theology of Luke-Acts." *CBQ* 31 (1969): 168–182. "The Early Church and the Hellenistic Synagogues." *ST* 37 (1973): 55–78.

Bornkamm, G. "Presbyteros." In *Theological Dictionary of the New Testament,* ed. Gerhard Kittel, trans. Geoffrey W. Bromiley, 10 vols. Grand Rapids: Eerdmans, 1964.

Bourke, Miles M. "Reflections on the Church Order in the New Testament." *CBQ* 30 (1968): 593–611.

Bouyer, Louis. "Dalla Liturgia Ebraica alla Liturgia Cristiana." *Communio* 64 (1982): 69–83.

______. "The Ecclesiastical Ministry and the Apostolic Succession." *Downside Review* 90 (1972): 133–144.

Brandon, S. G. F. *The Fall of Jerusalem and the Christian Church.* London, 1957.

Brandt, W. "Die Wortgruppe *leitourgeîn* im Hebräerbrief and bei Clemens Romanus." *Jahrbücher der Theologischen Schule.* Bethel, 1930. Pp. 145–176.

Brown, Raymond E. *New Testament Essays.* New York, 1965.

______. *Jesus, God and Man.* New York, 1967.

______. *Priest and Bishop: Biblical Reflections.* Paramus, 1970.

______. *Peter in the New Testament.* With Karl P. Donfreid and John Reumann, eds. New York, 1973.

______. *Biblical Reflections on Crises Facing the Church.* New York, 1975.

______. *The Community of the Beloved Disciple.* New York, 1979.

______. *The Critical Meaning of the Bible.* New York, 1981.

______ and John P. Meier. *Antioch and Rome.* New York, 1982.

______. *The Churches the Apostles Left Behind.* London, 1984.

Brunner, Gerbert. *Die theologische Mite des ersten Klemensbriefs.* Frankfurt am Main, 1972.

Buckland, W. W. *The Roman Law of Slavery*. Oxford, 1908.

Burghardt, Walter. "Apostolic Succession: Note on the Early Patristic Period." *Lutherans and Catholics in Dialogue*. Vol. 5: *Eucharist and Ministry*. Washington, 1970. Pp. 173–177.

Camelot, P. Th. *Lettres dignace d'Antioche*. Paris, 1969.

Campenhausen, Hans von. *Ecclesiastical Authority and Spiritual Power in the Church of the First Three Centuries*. Trans. J.A. Baker. Stanford, 1969. Pg. 139.

Cerfaux, Lucien. "Pour l'histoire du titre *apostolos* dans le Nouveau Testament." *Recueil L. Cerfaux*. Vol. 2. Gembloux, 1954. Pp. 185–200.

Chadwick, Henry. *The Early Church*. Harmondworth, 1967.

Chapman, John. "Clement I, Saint, Pope." *The Catholic Encyclopedia*. Vol. IV. New York, 1913. Pp. 12–17.

Citrini, T. "La ricerca su Simon Pietro: Traguardi e itinerari a trent'anni dal libro di Cullmann." *SC*, t. III. Torino, 1983. Pp. 512–556.

Clark, K. W. "Worship in the Jerusalem Temple after A. D. 70." *NTS* 6 (1960): 269–280.

Colson, Jean. *L'Evêque dans les communautés primitives. Tradition paulinienne et Tradition johannique de l'Episcopat, des origines à Saint Irénée*. Unam Sanctam 21. Paris, 1951.

Congar, Yves. "Inspiration des Ecritures canoniques et apostolicité de l'Eglise." *Revue des Sciences Philosophiques et Théologiques* 45 (1961): 32–42.

_____. "Composantes et idée de la Succession Apostolique." *Oecumenica* (1966): 61–80.

_____. "Eglise de Pierre, Eglise de Paul, Eglise de Jean. Destin d'un thème oecuménique." *The Ecumenical World of Orthodox Civilization. Russia and Orthodoxy*. Vol.III: *Essays in Honour of George Florovsky*. La Haye, 1973.

_____. *Diversity and Communion*. Trans. John Bowden. London, 1984.

Conzelmann, Hans. *History of Primitive Christianity*. Trans. John E. Steely. Nasvhille, 1973.

_____. "Luke's Place in the Development of Early Christianity." *Studies in Luke-Acts*. Martyn and Keck, eds. Nashville, 1966. Pp. 298–316.

_____. *The Theology of St. Luke*. Trans. G. Buswell. 2nd ed. New York, 1960.

_____. *An Outline of the Theology of the New Testament*. New York, 1969.

Cook, M. J. "Anti-Judaism in the New Testament." *Union Seminary Quarterly Review* 38 (1983): 125–137.

Cook, S. A., Adcock, F. E., and Charlesworth, M. P., eds. *The Cambridge Ancient History: The Augustan Empire 44 BC–AD 70*. Cambridge, 1966. Vol. XI: *The Imperial Peace*, reprinted with corrections, Cambridge, 1954.

Cooke, Bernard J. *Ministry to Word and Sacrament*. Philadelphia, 1976.

Creed, J. N. D. Kelly. *Early Christian Creeds*, 3rd ed. Singapore, 1972.

_____. *The Oxford Dictionary of Popes*. Oxford, 1986.

Cullmann, Oscar. "Les causes de la mort de Pierre et Paul d'après le témoignage de Clément Romain." *Revue d'Histoire et de Philosophie religieuse* 10 (1930): 294–300.

_____. *Peter: Disciple, Apostle, Martyr*. Trans. Floyd V. Filson. Philadelphia, 1953.

Danielou, Jean. "Review of *Clemens Romanus and der Frühkatholizismus in I Clemens 1–7* (by K. Beyschlag)." *Recherches de Science Religieuse* 54 (1966): 276–280.

_____. *Théologie du Judéo-Christianisme*. Tournai, 1958.

_____. *A History of Early Christian Doctrine: Vol. III: The Origins of Latin Christianity*. Trans. David Smith and John Austin Baker. London, 1968.

de Lubac, Henri. *Eglises particulières et église universelle*. Rome, 1971.

de Vaux, Roland. "Le Temple de Jérusalem." *Bible et Orient*. Paris, 1967. Pp. 303–315.

_____. *Ancient Israel: Its Life and Institutions*. Trans. John McHugh. London, 1961.

Dillon, R. J. "Ministry as Stewardship of the Tradition in the New Testament." In *Catholic Theology Society of American Proceedings* (1969). Pp. 10–62.

Donfried, Karl P. ed. *The Romans Debate*. Minneapolis, 1977.

Duchesne, L., ed. *Liber Pontificalis*. Paris, 1886–1892.

Dupont, Jacques. "Le nom d'apôtres a-t-il été donné aux Douze par Jésus?" *L'Orient syrien* 1 (1956): 267–290.

Edgar, S. L. "Respect for Context in Quotations from the Old Testament." *NTS* 9 (1962–1963): 55–62.

Edmundson, George. "The Chureh in Rome in the First Century." *The Bampton Lectures for 1913*. London, 1913.

Ehrhard, A. *Urkirche and Frühkatholizismus*. Bonn, 1935.

Elliott, John H. *The Elect and the Holy*. Leiden, 1966.

_____. *A Home for the Homeless*. Philadelphia, 1981.

_____. "A Catholie Gospel: Reflections on Early Catholicism in the New Testament." *CBQ* 31 (1969): 213–223.

_____. "Ministry and Chureh Order in the New Testament: A Traditio-Historical Analysis (1 Peter 5:1–5)." *CBQ* 32 (1970): 367–391.

Ellis, E. E. *Eschatology in Luke*. Philadelphia, 1972.

_____. "Present and Future Eschatology in Luke." *NTS* 12 (1965–1966): 27–41.

Eusebius of Caesarea. *The Ecclesiastical History*. Vols. I and II. Trans. H. J. Lawlor. Cambridge, 1964.

Farmer, William R. and Farkasfalvy, Denis M. *The Formation of the New Testament Canon*. New York, 1983.

Ferrua, A. "Filocalo, l'amante delle belle lettere." *Civilta Cattolica* 1 (1939): 31–47.

_____. "Epigrammata Damasiana." *Sussidi allo studio delle antichita cristiane* 2 (1942): 21–35.

Finkelstein, Louis, "The Birhat-ha-Mazon." *Jewish Quarterly Review* 19 (1928–1929): 211–262.

Fitzmyer, Joseph. *The Gospel According to Luke I–IX*. New York, 1981. Vol. II: Luke X–XXIV, New York, 1985.

Frend, W. H. C. *Martyrdom and Persecution in the Early Church*. Oxford, 1965.

Fuellenbach, John. *Ecclesiastical Office and the Primacy of Rome: An Evaluation of Recent Theological Discussion of First Clement*. Washington, DC, 1980.

Fuller, Reginald H. *The Foundations of New Testament Christology*. London, 1969.

_____. "Early Catholicism: An Anglican Reaction to a German Debate." *Festschrift E. Schweizer*. Pp. 34–41.

_____. *The New Testament in Current Study*. New York, 1962.

Gager, John G. *Kingdom and Community: The Social World of Early Christianity*. Englewood Cliffs, 1975.

_____. "Social Description and Sociological Explanation in the Study of Early Christianity: A Review Essay." In *The Bible and Literature*, ed. W. K. Gottwald. Nashville, pp. 428–470.

Gamsey, Peter. *Social Status and Legal Privilege in the Roman Empire*. Oxford, 1970.

Garzetti, A. *From Tiberius to the Antonines*. London, 1974.

Gassmann, Gunther. "Die Entwicklung der ökomenischen Diskussion über das Amt." *Okomenische Rundschau* 22 (1973): 454–468.

Gaudemet, J. *L'Eglise dans l'Empire Romain*. Paris, 1958.

Giblet, Jean. "I presbyteri collaboratori dell'ordine episcopale." *La Chiesa del Vaticano* II, ed. Guillherme Barauna. Florence, 1966. Pp. 872–895.

Grant, Michael. *The Roman Forum*. London, 1970.

_____. *The Roman Emperors.* Oxford, 1974.

Grant, Robert M. *Eusebius as Church Historian.* Oxford, 1980.

Grech, Prosper. "Timoteo Tito: Modelli del Vescovo nel Periodo subapostolico." *Il Ministero Ordinato nel Dialogo Ecumenico, Scritti in onore di Gerardo Bekes.* Rome, 1985.

Grelot, Pierre. *Les Poèmes du Serviteur.* Paris, 1981.

Gy, P. M. "Remarques sur le vocabulaire antique du sacerdoce chrétien." *Etudes sur le Sacrement de l'Ordre.* Paris, 1957. Pp. 125–145.

Haenchen, E. *The Acts of the Apostles: A Commentary.* Philadelphia, 1971.

Hahn, Ferdinand. *The Titles of Jesus in Christology: Their History in Early Christianity.* London, 1969.

_____. "Das Problem des Frühkatholizismus." *Theologisches Jahrbuch* 1983. Leipzig, 1983.

_____. "Das apostolische and das nachapostolische Zeitalter als Ökomenisches Problem." *Theologisches Jahrbuch* 1983. Leipzig, 1983.

Halton, T. "Hegissipus in Eusebius." *Studia Patristica* XVIII/2. Pp. 688–693 .

Hardy, E. R. "The Decline and Fall of the Confessor-Presbyter." *Studia Patristica* XV. Pp. 221–225.

Harnack, Adolf von. *The Constitution and Law of the Church of the First Two Centuries.* London, 1910.

_____. *Einführung in die alten Kirchengeschichte: das Schreiben der römischen Kirche an die Korinthische.* Leipzig, 1929.

Hatch, E. *The Organization of Early Christian Churches.* London, 1881.

Henderson, B. W. *Five Roman Emperors.* London, 1978.

Henry, P. "Why Is Contemporary Scholarship So Enamored of Ancient Heretics?" *Studia Patristica* XVII/1. Pp. 123–126.

Hertling, L. von. "1 Kor 16,15 und I Clem 42." *Biblica* 20 (1939): 276–283.

Hiers, R. H. "The Problem of the Delay of the Parousia in Luke-Acts." *NTS* 20 (1973–1974): 145–155.

Hübner, Reinhard M. "Die Anfänge von Diakonat, Presbyterat und Episkopat in der frühen Kirche." In *Das Priestertum in der einen Kirche.* Albert Rauch and Paul Imhof, eds. Aschaffenburg, 1987.

Jaubert, Annie. *Clement de Rome: Epître aux Corinthiens.* Paris, 1971.

_____. "Les sources de la conception militaire de l'Eglise en I Clément 37." *VC* 18 (1964): 74–84.

_____. "Thèmes lévitiques dans la Prima Clementis." *VC* 18 (1964): 193–203.

Javierre, A. M. "La successione apostolica nel dialogo ecumenico attomo al ministero." In *Baptême, Ministrie, Ministère. Réflexions de Théologiens catholiques sur le document oecuménique, "La réconciliation des Eglises."* Rome, 1977. Pp. 185–247.

Jay, Eric G. "From Presbyter-Bishops to Bishops and Presbyters." The Second Century I (1981): 125–162.

Jeremias, Joachim. *Jerusalem in the Time of Jesus.* Trans. F. H. and C. H. Cave. Philadelphia, 1969.

Jervell, J. "*The Acts of the Apostles and the History of Early Christianity.*" *ST* 37 (1983): 17–32.

Jones, Brian W. *The Emperor Titus.* London, 1984.

Josephus, Flavius. *The Jewish War.* Trans. H. St. J. Thackeray. Cambridge, 1968.

______. *The Jewish Antiquities.* Trans. H. St. J. Thackeray. Cambridge, 1967.

Jourjon, M. "Remarques sur le vocabulaire sacerdotal de la Ia Clementis." *Epektasis; Melánges J. Daniélou.* Ed. J. Fontaine. Paris, 1972. Pp. 107–110.

Jurgens, Wiliam A. *The Faith of the Early Fathers.* Vol. I. Collegeville, 1970.

______. *The Priesthood.* Trans. W. A. Jurgens of *Peri Hierosynes* of St. John Chrysostom. New York, 1955.

Karrer, Otto. "Successione Apostolica e Primato." *Problemi e Orientamenti di Teologia Dommatica.* Ed. Carlo Marzorati. Milano, 1957. Pp. 253–302.

______. "Ministry and Community in the New Testament." *SBT* 41 (London, 1964): 63–94.

______. "Unity and Diversity in New Testament Ecclesiology." *New Testament* 6 (1963): 290–297.

Kasper, Walter. *An Introduction to Christian Faith.* Trans. V. Green. New York, 1980.

Keck, L. E. and Martyn, J. L., eds. *Studies in Luke-Acts: Essays Presented in Honor of Paul Schubert.* Nashville, 1966.

Kent, John Harvey. *Corinth* VIII/3. *The Inscriptions,* 1926–1950. Princeton, 1966.

Kenyon, Kathleen M. *Digging up Jerusalem.* London, 1974.

Knoch, Otto. *Eigenart und Bedeutung der Eschatologie im theologischen Aufriss des ersten Clemensbriefes.* Bonn, 1964.

Koester, Helmut. *Introduction to the New Testament.* Vol.II: *History and Literature of Early Christianity.* Philadelphia, 1983.

Kretschmar, Georg. "Frühkatholizismus. Die Beurteilung theologischer Entwicklungen im späten ersten und zweiten Jahrhundert nach Christus." *Theologisches Jahrbuch* 1983. Leipzig, 1983.

Kummel, Werner Georg. "*Notwendigkeit und Grenze des nt. Kanons.*" *ZTK* (1950): 272–276.

_____. *Promise and Fulfillment: The Eschatological Message of Jesus*. Trans. Dorothea M. Barton. London, 1957.

_____. "Futurische und präsentische Eschatologie im ältesten Christentum." *NTS* 5 (1958–1959): 113–126.

_____. *Introduction to the New Testament*. Trans. Howard Clark Kee, 17th ed. Nashville, 1975.

Küng, Hans. "What Is the Essence of Apostolic Succession?" In *Apostolic Succession: Rethinking a Barrier to Unity*, Concilium 34. New York, 1968.

_____. *The Church*. Trans. Ray and Rosaleen Ockenden. New York, 1967.

Lampe, G. W. H. "Some Notes on the Significance of *Basileia tou Theou,Basileia Christou.*" *JTS* 49 (1948): 58–73.

Lampe, Pete. "Die stadtrömischen Christen in den ersten beiden Jahrhunderten." WUNT 2; Reihe 18. Tubingen, 1987.

Lanne, Emmanuel. "Convergence on the Ordained Ministry." *Ecumenical Perspectives on Baptism, Eucharist and Ministry*. Ed. Max Thurian. Geneva, 1983. Pp. 119–128.

Lécuyer, J. "Episcopat et presbytérat dans les écrits d'Hippolyte de Rome." *Recherches de Science Religieuse* 41 (1953): 30–50.

Lehmann, Karl. "Das dogmatische Problem des theologischen Ansatzes zum Verständnis des Amtspriestertums." *Existenzprobleme des Priesters*. Ed. Franz Henrich. Munchen, 1969. Pp. 123–175.

Lewis, Naphali and Reinhold, Meyer, eds. *Roman Civilization*. Vol. II: *The Empire*. New York, 1955.

Lightfoot, J. B. *The Apostolic Fathers*. Vol. 1: Part 1. London, 1890.

Lohse, E. *The First Christians, Their Writings and Beliefs*. Trans. M. E. Borig. Philadelphia, 1982.

Maccarone, M. *Vicarius Christi: Storia del Titolo Papale*. Roma, 1952.

Marshall, I. H. "'Early Catholicism' in the New Testament." In *New Dimensions in New Testament Study*. Eds. R. N. Lonenecker and M. C. Tenney. Grand Rapids, 1974. Pp. 217–231.

Marxen, W. "Der Frühkatholizismus im Neuen Testament." Bib S (N) 21. Neukirchen, 1958.

Mattingly, H. and Sydenham, R. *The Roman Imperial Coinage*, II. Oxford, 1955.

Mazar, B. *The Excavations in the Old City of Jerusalem*. Jerusalem, 1969.

McCue, James F. "The Roman Primacy in the Patristic Period: the Beginnings through Nicea." *Papal Primacy and the Universal Church, Lutherans and Catholics in Dialogue.* Vol. V. Ed. Paul C. Empie and T. Austin Murphy. Minneapolis, 1974.

Meeks, Wayne A. *The First Urban Christians: The Social World of the Apostle Paul.* New Haven, 1983.

Metzger, B. *Les Constitutions Apostoliques.* Paris, 1984.

Miles, M. F. "Ignatius and the Church." *Studia Patristica,* XVII. Oxford, 1982. Pp. 750–755.

Moingt, J. "Authority and Ministry." *Journal of Ecumenical Studies* 19 (1982): 202–225.

Molina, Bruce. *The New Testament World: Insights from Cultural Anthropology.* London, 1983.

Momigliano, A. *Essays on Ancient and Modern Historiography.* Oxford, 1977.

Mommsen, T. *Über den Chronographen im Jahre* 354. Berlin, 1850.

Morris, L. *The Gospel According to St. Luke: An Introduction and Commentary.* Grand Rapids, 1974.

Moulton, J. H. *A Grammar of New Testament Greek.* Vol. VI: Style. Trans. Nigel Turner. Edinburgh, 1976. Vol. III: Syntax. Edinburgh, 1963.

Munck, J. "Paul the Apostle and the Twelve." *ST* 3 (1950–1951): 96–110.

Munro, W. *Authority in Paul and Peter: The Identification of a Pastoral Stratum in the Pauline Corpus and I Peter.* Cambridge, 1983.

Murphy-O'Connor, Jerome. *I Corinthians.* Wilmington, 1979.

______. *St. Paul's Corinth.* Wilmington, 1983.

______. "Review of *Antioch and Rome* (by R. Brown and J. Meier)." *Revue Biblique* 91 (1984): 146.

Mussner, F. "Frühkatholizismus." *LTK* 6 (1961): 89–90.

Neufeld, Karl H. "Frühkatholizismus - Idee and Begriff." *Theologisches Jahrbuch* 1983. Leipzig, 1983.

Noll, R. R. "The Search for a Christian Ministerial Priesthood in 1 Clement." *Studia Patristica* XIII. Berlin, 1975.

Norris, Frederick W. "Ignatius, Polycarp and 1 Clement: Walter Bauer Reconsidered." *VC* 30 (1976): 23–44.

Osborn, C. D. "The Historical Present in Mark as a Text Critical Criterion." *Biblica* 64 (1983): 486–500.

Pagels, Elaine. *The Gnostic Gospels.* New York, 1979.

Pittenger, Norman. *Christian Faith and the Question of History*. Philadelphia, 1973.

Powell, D. "Ordo Presbyterii." *JTS* 26 (1975): 290–328.

Quinn, Jerome D. "Ministry in the New Testament." *Lutherans and Catholics in Dialogue*. Vol. IV. Washington DC, 1970. Pp. 69–100.

______. "New Testament Data on Priestly Ordination." *America* (September 6, 1980): 94–97.

______. "Ordination in the Pastoral Epistles." *Communio* 8 (1980): 358–369.

Rahner, Karl and Ratzinger, Joseph. *The Episcopate and the Primacy*. Trans. K. Baker. New York, 1962.

______. "On the Relationship Between the Pope and the College of Bishops." *Theological Investigations*. Vol. 10. Pp. 50–70.

Rajak, Tessa. *Josephus: The Historian and His Society*. London, 1983.

Ratzinger, Joseph. "La Collegialità episcopale dal Punto di Vista Teologico." *La Chiesa del Vaticano II*. Ed. Guilherme Barauna. Florence, 1965. Pp. 733–760.

______. "The Pastoral Implications of Episcopal Collegiality." *Concilium* 1. Glen Rock, 1964. Pp. 39–67.

______. "Opfer, Sakrament und Priestertum in der Entwicklung der Kirche." *Catholica* 26 (1972): 108–125.

______. *Eschatologie - Tod und ewiges Leben*. Regensburg, 1977.

Reynders, R. "Paradosis: le progrès de l'idée de Tradition jusqu'à S. Irénée." *Recherches de Théologie ancienne et médiévale* 5 (1933): 161–162.

Rigaux, Beda. "St. Peter in Comtemporary Exegesis." Trans. John Drury. *Concilium* 27. New York, 1967. Pp. 147–179.

______. "The Twelve Apostles." *Concilium* 34. New York, 1968.

Robinson, James M. and Koester, Helmut. *Trajectories through Early Christianity*. Philadelphia, 1971.

Robinson, John A. T. *Redating the New Testament*. London, 1976.

______. "The Most Primitive Christology of All?" *JTS* 7 (1956): 177–189.

Rohde, J. "Häresie und Schisma im ersten Clemensbrief und in den Ignatiusbriefen." *New Testament* 10 (1968): 217–233.

Rollman, Hans. "Paulus alienus: William Wrede on Comparing Jesus and Paul." In *Studies in Honour of Francis Wright Beare*. Eds. John C. Hurd and Peter Richardson. Waterloo, 1984. Pp. 23–45.

Rordorf, Willi. "Une nouvelle édition de la Didaché." *Studia Patristica* XV. Berlin, 1984. Pp. 26–30.

Sanders, E. P. *Paul and Palestinian Judaism*. Philadelphia, 1977.

Schlier, Heinrich. "Grundelemente des Priesterlichen Amtes im Neuen Testament." *Theologie und Philosophie* 11 (1969): 161–180.

Schmitals, Walter. *The Office of Apostle in the Early Church*. Trans. John E. Steely. Nashville, 1969.

Schmitz, Herman-Josef. *Frühkatholizismus bei Adolf von Harnack, Rudolph Sohm und Ernst Kasemann*. Düsseldorf, 1977.

Schnackenburg, Rudolph. *The Church in the New Testament*. London, 1974.

______. "Apostles before and during Paul's Time." *Apostolic History and the Gospel: Biblical and Historical Essays Presented to F. F. Bruce on His 60th Birthday*. Eds. W. W. Gasque and R[alph] P. Martin. Grand Rapids, 1970. Pp. 287–303.

Schmidt, Joel. *Vie et Mort des esclaves dans la Rome antique*. Paris, 1973.

Schneiders, Sandra M. "Theological Trends: Ministry and Ordination." *The Way* 20 (1980): 290–299.

Schoedel, W. "Are the Letters of Ignatius of Antioch Authentic?" *Religious Studies Review* 6 (1980): 196–201.

______. *Ignatius of Antioch: A Commentary on the Letters*. Phliadelphia, 1985.

Scobie, H. H. "Jesus or Paul? The Origin of the Universal Mission of the Christian Church." *From Jesus to Paul: Studies in Honour of Francis Wright Beare*. Eds. John C. Hurd and Peter Richardson. Waterloo, 1984. Pp. 47–60.

Schussler-Fiorenza, Elizabeth. *In Memory of Her*. London, 1983.

Scroggs, R. "The Sociological Interpretation of the New Testament." *NTS* (1980): 164–179.

Senior, Donald. *The Passion of Jesus in the Gospel of Mark*. Wilmington, 1984.

______. *The Passion of Jesus in the Gospel of Matthew*. Wilmington, 1985.

Seppelt, F. X. *Geschichte der Päpste*. Munich, 1954–1959.

Sherwin-White, A. N. *The Roman Citizenship*, 2nd ed. Oxford, 1973.

Siari, Antonio. "Perché i Vescovi possono obbedire allo Spirito." *Communio* 53 (1980): 4–17.

Siebgen, Hermann J. *VOCES: eine Bibliographie zu Worten and Begriffen aus der Patristik* (1918–1978). Berlin, 1979.

Smith, Morton. "The Report about Peter in 1 Clem. V. 4." *NTS* 7 (1960): 86–88.

Smith, T. V. *Petrine Controversies in Early Christianity: Attitudes towards Peter in Christian Writings of the First Two Centuries*. Tubingen, 1985.

Soggin, J. Alberto. *A History of Israel from the Beginnings to the Bar Kochba Revolt, A.D. 135*. London, 1984.

Sohm, Rudolf. *Kirchenrecht*. Leipzig, 1892. Reprinted, 1923.

Stephenson, J. *A New Eusebius: Documents Illustrative of the History of the Church to A.D. 337*. London, 1957.

Stem, Henry. Le *Calendrier de 354: étude sur son texte et ses illustrations*. Paris, 1953.

Telfer, W. *The Office of a Bishop*. London, 1962.

Talbert, C. H. "Shifting Sands: The Recent Study of the Gospel of Luke." *Int*. 30 (1976): 381–395.

Testini, Pasquale. *Archeologia Cristiana*, 2nd ed. Bari, 1980.

Theissen, Gerd. *Essays on Corinth: The Social Setting of Pauline Christianity*. Ed. and trans. J. H. Schutz. Edinburgh, 1982.

Thyen, H. *Der Stil der Jüdisch-Hellenistische Homelie*. Göttingen, 1955.

Troeltsch, Ernst. "Über historische and dogmatische Methode in der Theologie." *Gesammelte Schriften*. Vol. II. Tübingen, 1913. Pp. 729–753.

______. *The Social Teaching of the Christian Churches*. New York, 1931.

Vanhoye, Albert. "Sacerdoce commun et sacerdoce ministériel: distinction et rapports." *Nouvelle Revue Théologique* 97 (1975): 193–207.

______. *Prêtres Anciens, Prêtre Nouveau selon le Nouveau Testament*. Paris, 1980.

Van Unnik, W. C. "Is 1 Clement 20 Purely Stoic?" *VC* 4 (1950): 181–189.

Vielhauer, Philipp. *Geschichte der urchristlichen Literatur*. Berlin, 1975.

______. "On the 'Paulinism' in Acts." *Studies in Luke-Acts*. Eds. L. Keck and J. L. Martyn. New York, 1966. Pp. 33–50.

Wagner, Harald. "An der Ursprüngen des frühkatholischen Problems. Die Ortsbestimmung des Katholizismus im älteren Luthertum." *Frankfurter Theologische Studien* 14 (1972).

Weber, Max. *The Sociology of Religion*. Trans. E. Fischoff. Boston, 1963. Welborn, L. L. "On the Date of First Clement." *Journal of the Chicago Society of Biblical Research* 29 (1984): 35–54.

Wellesley, K. *The Long Year, A.D. 69*. London, 1975.

White, J. L. "St. Paul and the Apostolic Letter Tradition." *CBQ* 45 (1983): 433–444.

Wilhelm-Hooijbergh, A. E. "A Different View of Clemens Romanus." *Heythrop Journal* 16 (1975): 266–288.

Wilken, Robert L. *The Christians as the Romans Saw Them*. New Haven, 1984.

Wilson, S.G. "From Jesus to Paul: The Contours and Consequences of a Debate." *From Jesus to Paul: Studies in Honour of Francis Wright Beare*. Eds. John C. Hurd and Peter Richardson. Waterloo, 1984. Pp. 1–21.

Wright, Addison. "The Widow's Mites: Praise or Lament? A Matter of Contexts." *CBQ* 44 (1981): 256–265.

Zizioulas, J. "Épiskopè et Épiskopos dans l'Église primitive. Bref inventoire de la documentation." *Irénikon* 6 (1983): 484–502.

4. *Miscellaneous*

Annuario Pontificio, 1988. Libreria Editrice Vaticana, 1988.

The Priestly Ministry: Report of the International Theological Commission. Trans. of *Le Ministère Sacerdotal* (by James Depuis, SJ). Bangalore, 1971.

The Codex Sinaiticus and the Codex Alexandrinus. Published by The Trustees of the British Museum. London, 1963.

Baptism, Eucharist and Ministry. Faith and Order Paper No. III. World Council of Churches. Geneva, 1982.

Letter of the Congregation for the Doctrine of the Faith on Certain Questions Concerning Eschatology. AAS, LXXI (1979): 939ff.

Declaration of the Congregation for the Doctrine of the Faith on the Admission of Women to the Priesthood. AAS, LXIX (1977): 981ff.